# Italian Country Inns & Villas

## BOOKS IN KAREN BROWN'S COUNTRY INN SERIES

# Italian Country Inns & Villas

CLARE BROWN, CTC

Illustrated by

BARBARA TAPP

Karen Brown's Country Inn Series

Travel Press
San Mateo, California

TRAVEL PRESS editors: Clare Brown, CTC, Karen Brown, June Brown, CTC, Iris Sandilands

Illustrations: Barbara Tapp
Maps: Keith Cassell
Cover painting: "Domingo" (Cesare Rebesco)

This book is written in cooperation with:
Town and Country - Hillsdale Travel
16 East Third Avenue, San Mateo, California 94401

This Warner Books edition is published by arrangement with Travel Press, San Mateo, California 94401

Warner Books, Inc., 666 Fifth Avenue, New York, NY 10103
Ⓦ A Warner Communications Company

Printed in the United States of America
First Warner Books Trade Paperback Printing: March 1988
10 9 8 7 6 5 4 3 2 1

**LIBRARY OF CONGRESS**
**Library of Congress Cataloging-in-Publication Data**

Brown, Karen.
    Italian country inns and villas / Karen Brown.
        p.   cm.
    Includes index.
    ISBN 0-446-38809-2 (pbk.) (U.S.A.) / 0-446-38955-2(pbk.) (Canada)
    1. Hotels, taverns, etc. ·· Italy ·· Guide-books. 2. Italy-
-Description and travel ·· 1975 ·· Guide-books. I. Title.
TX910.I8B76 1988
647 .944501 ·· dc19                              87027213
                                                       CIP

*To My Best Friend, Bill*

*With Love and Gratitude for*

*Many Miles of Memories*

# Contents

HOTEL SECTION

# Foreword

As we go to press with this third edition of *Italian Country Inns & Villas,* we are truly pleased to include 36 new inns to make your holiday even more special. These additions are some of the most charming small hotels in Italy - many of which are rarely found in other travel guides. A few of these new hotels are ones we happened upon while combing the backroads, others are recommendations from hoteliers, but some of our favorites are those you found and shared with us. Not only is this guide strengthened by your suggestions for new hotels, but also by your criticisms. We have dropped hotels that did not maintain the standards of comfort, hospitality and charm we want you to experience in your travels. Thank you for sharing your adventures - we truly appreciate your taking the time to write or call. We promise to always inspect every hotel we recommend and, with your help, continue to present you with the finest small hotels throughout Europe.

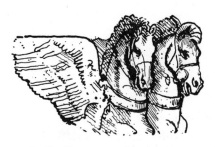 *Introduction*

Of all the countries in the world, none is more magical than Italy: truly a tourist's paradise - a traveller's dream destination. No one could be so blase that within Italy's narrow boot there would not be something to tantalize his fancy. For the archaeologist, there are some of the most fascinating and perfectly preserved ancient monuments existing today - just begging to be explored. For the gourmet, there is probably the best food in the world. For the outdoorsman, there are towering mountains to conquer and magnificent ski slopes to sample. For the lover of art, the museums are bursting with the genius of Italy's sons such as Michelangelo, Leonardo da Vinci, and Raphael. For the architect, Italy is a school of design - you are surrounded by the ancient buildings whose perfection has inspired the styles of today. For the history buff, Italy is a joy of wonders - her cities are veritable living museums where you are surrounded by the ghosts of Caesar. For the wine connoisseur, Italy produces an unbelievable selection of wine whose quality is unsurpassed. For the adventurer, Italy has intriguing medieval walled villages tucked away in every part of the country just waiting to be explored. For the beach buff, Italy's lakes and islands hold promise of some of the most elegant resorts in the world. For the religious pilgrim, Italy is the cradle of much of the world's faith and home of some of the world's greatest saints. The miracle of Italy is that all these treasures come "packaged" in a gorgeous country of majestic mountains, misty lakes, idyllic islands, wonderful walled villages and gorgeous cities. Plus, the climate is ideal and the people warm and gracious. Italy is truly a delightful destination.

# ABOUT THIS GUIDE

This guide is written with two main objectives: to describe the most romantic small hotels throughout Italy and to "tie" these hotels together with itineraries that include enough details so the traveller can plan his own holiday.

This introduction explains how to use the guide and also touches upon what to expect while travelling. After the introduction comes the main part of the guide which is divided into two sections. The first section outlines itineraries with sightseeing suggestions along the way and a hotel featured for each night's stay. The second section of the book has two parts. First is a complete list of hotels we have personally inspected, appearing alphabetically by town with a brief description, an illustration and pertinent information provided for each. Second is a list of hotels recommended by our readers. The hotels featured in our guide vary tremendously: some are deluxe, grand hotels fit for a king and very expensive; others are quite simple little cottages tucked away in remote hamlets and priced to accommodate any budget. We include them all if they have "personality", charm and an antique ambiance. There are a few hotels which are included that do not quite live up to the criterion of "old-world charm": the reason they have been included is because in their particular area there just were no "perfect" choices, and since we felt you might need a place to stay, we tried to find the very best possibility.

# CURRENT

You will need a transformer plus an adapter if you plan to use an American-made electrical appliance in Italy. The voltage is usually 220, but sometimes it varies and is 115 or 125. Check with the manager of the hotel before plugging anything into an electrical outlet. Frequently the larger hotels can loan you a properly adapted electric hairdryer or razor.

# DRIVING

*DRIVER'S LICENSE:* Although it is not mandatory, we suggest obtaining an international driver's license before driving in Italy. Should you have any problems along the way, it is more efficient to show your international card which is easily understood overseas.

*GASOLINE:* Gasoline is very expensive so plan ahead and budget this as part of your trip if you are driving. If you purchase a car in Europe and it is registered in a country other than Italy, you can buy gas discount coupons at the border.

*ROADS:* The Italian roads are nothing short of spectacular. You will discover some of the finest highways in the world. In fact, the Italians are absolute geniuses when it comes to their engineering feats (which actually is not surprising when you think what a fantastic road system the Romans built two thousand years ago). Nothing seems to daunt them. You would think the mountains were of clay instead of solid rock, the way they tunnel through them for miles on end. When it comes to roads nothing seems to be too expensive or too much trouble. Sometimes a roadway will be seemingly suspended forever in mid air, as it bridges a mountain crevasse.

*TOLL ROADS:* Italy has a network of super expressways that draws the whole country into an easily manageable destination by car. Once you are on the toll roads the miles whip by and you can go quickly from almost any area of Italy to another most efficiently. However, be forewarned: these toll roads are very expensive. It seems that about every half hour a toll station appears and you owe another couple of dollars. But it is worth it. Every cent is well spent when you consider the alternative of creeping along within a maze of trucks and buzzing motorcycles taking forever to go only a few miles. Take the toll roads for the major distances you need to cover, and then choose the small roads when you wish to meander leisurely through the countryside.

The toll roads are a little confusing until you learn the system - even then it is confusing because just when you think you have the operation "down pat" you will find it varies slightly. But this is the most common routine: first follow the green expressway signs toward the toll road. Sometimes these signs begin miles from the road so be patient and continue the game of "follow the sign". Each entrance to the expressway handles traffic going in both directions. As you enter into the toll gate there is usually a red button you push and a card pops out of a slot. After going through the toll station you choose the direction you want to go. Leaving the expressway there will be a toll station where your ticket will be collected and you will pay according to how many miles traveled.

*ROAD SIGNS:* Before starting on the road prepare yourself by learning the international driving signs so that you can obey all the rules of the road and avoid the embarrassment of heading the wrong way down a small street or parking in a forbidden area! There are several basic sign shapes. The triangular signs warn that there is danger ahead. The circular signs indicate compulsory rules and information. The square signs give information concerning telephones, parking, camping, etc. To acquaint you, some of the more common signs are listed below.

| No entry for pedestrians | No animals | No entry for all motor vehicles | End of no overtaking | No overtaking for lorries | End of no overtaking |
| Danger! Level crossing | Low-flying aircraft | Falling rocks | Cross-wind | Quayside or river bank | Two-way traffic |
| Give way | Slippery road | Uneven road | Steep hill – descent | Tunnel | Opening bridge |

*Introduction*

End of all restrictions
 Halt sign
 Halt sign
 Customs
 No stopping
 No parking/waiting

 Mechanical help
 Filling station
 Telephone
 Camping site
 Caravan site
 Youth hostel

 All vehicles prohibited
 No entry for all vehicles
 No right turn
 No U-turns
 No entry for motorcars
 No overtaking

 Road works
 Loose chippings
 Level crossing with barrier
 Level crossing without barrier
 Maximum speed limit
 End of speed limit

 Traffic signals ahead
 Pedestrians
 Children
 Animals
 Wild animals
 Other dangers

 Intersection with non-priority road
 Merging traffic from left
 Merging traffic from right
 Road narrows
 Road narrows at left
 Road narrows at right

# FOOD and DRINK

It is almost impossible to get a bad meal in Italy. Italians themselves love to eat and seem to make dining a social occasion to be with family and friends, so the restaurants are filled not only with tourists but with the Italians who dawdle at the tables long after the meal is over, chatting and laughing with perhaps a glass of wine or a last cup of coffee.

You will soon get in the spirit of the game of deciding which kind of restaurant to choose for your next meal - and the selection is immense, all the way from the simple family trattoria where mama is cooking in the kitchen to the most elegant of gourmet restaurants with world renowned chefs. Whichever you choose, you will not be disappointed.

The Italians are artists when it comes to pasta, seen on every menu and prepared in endless, fascinating, delicious ways. Wine of course is served with every meal. You rarely see an Italian family eating without their bottle of wine on the table. Unless you are a true wine connoisseur I suggest the regional wines. If you ask your waiter to assist you with the choice, you will flatter him and discover many superb wines. Some of the most popular wines which you will see on the Italian menus are: CHIANTI, a popular wine produced in the Tuscany area south of Florence; MARSALA, a golden sweet wine from Sicily; SOAVE, a superb light wine produced near Venice; ORVIETO, a semi-sweet wine from the Umbria area near Assisi, and EST EST EST, a beautiful semi-sweet wine produced near Rome. The story that I heard about the last wine, Est Est Est, is lots of fun and perhaps even true. It seems that a wealthy man was travelling south and, being a true gourmet both of food and drink, he sent his servant before him to pick out all the best places to eat along the way. When the servant neared Rome he found such a divine wine that all he could relay back to his master was EST EST EST, which as you students of Latin will remember means Yes Yes Yes! And the wine is definitely still "Yes Yes Yes" as are most that you will enjoy drinking in Italy!

## HOTELS - BASIS FOR SELECTION

This guide does not try to appeal to everyone. It is definitely prejudiced - the hotels included are ones we have seen and liked. It might be a splendid villa elegantly positioned overlooking one of Italy's romantic lakes or a simple little chalet snuggled high in a mountain meadow. But there is a common denominator - they all have charm. Therefore, if you too prefer to travel spending your nights in romantic old villas, charming little chalets, dramatic medieval castles, ancient monasteries, converted peasants' cottages and gorgeous palaces...then we are kindred souls and you can follow the paths we have suggested and each night will be an adventure.

For some of you, cost will not be a factor if the hotel is outstanding. For others, budget will guide your choices. The appeal of a simple little inn with rustic wooden furniture will beckon some, while the glamor of ornate ballrooms dressed with crystal chandeliers and gilded mirrors will appeal to others. What we have tried to do is to indicate what each hotel has to offer, and describe the setting, so that you can make the choice to suit your own preferences and holiday. We feel if you know what to expect, you will not be disappointed, so we have tried to be candid and honest in our appraisals. Also, some hotels are ideal for children while others are definitely adult oriented. We have indicated these special situations under the hotel descriptions.

## HOTELS - COST

The price for a room in Italy has soared. The greatest complaint in the last edition of our Italian guide was from readers who called to say, "Why didn't you warn us about the price of the hotel?" The reason why what we had estimated to be a "moderately priced" hotel became suddenly a "very expensive" hotel was not because of a sudden enormous inflation, but rather because the dollar had slipped so desperately in relation to the lire. To solve this problem, we are returning to our original system of giving the room rate in Italian lire.

## HOTELS - CREDIT CARDS

Many small hotels do not accept credit cards. Those hotels which do accept "plastic payment" are indicated in the hotel description section using the following abbreviations: AX - American Express, VS - Visa, MC - Master Charge, DC - Diner's Club, or simply - All major.

## HOTELS - DECOR

Hotels usually reflect a rather formal, sometimes fussy ambiance. In a few instances (which we note in the hotel descriptions) the hotels display a country cozy mood, but this is not the norm. When antiques are used, they are frequently the fancy, gilded variety.

## HOTELS - HOW TO INTERPRET THE RATE

In the hotel reference section in the back of the book each hotel will show a rate which will reflect the approximate cost for two persons including tax, service and Continental breakfast. There are a few hotels where breakfast and one other meal (either lunch or dinner) is included in the rate and, if so, this too is noted. Please use the rates given only as a general ballpark guide because each hotel has such a wide range of price possibilities that it is impossible to project completely accurately. Also, each year there is some inflation. However, the lire price given will help you anticipate what the approximate cost will be. When you begin to plan your holiday, check with your bank to see the current exchange rate. Hopefully the dollar will become stronger and travelling in Italy will again become a bargain.

## HOTELS - HOW TO ECONOMIZE

For those of you who want to squeeze the most value out of each night's stay, we have several suggestions:

1) Travel off season - spring and fall are usually lovely in Italy and the hotels often have bargain rates.

2) Ask for a room without a private bathroom - many hotels have very nice rooms, usually with a washbasin in the room, but with the bathroom "down the hall".

3) Ask if there is a weekly rate - frequently hotels will offer a price break for guests staying a week or more.

4) If travelling with children, ask if there is a special family suite at a lesser price than separate rooms.

5) Ask about rates with meals included - if staying for three days or longer, many hotels offer a special rate including meals: MAP (Modified American Plan) means two meals a day are included, AP (American Plan) means three meals a day are included.

6) Last, but not least, is the most important way to save money. Stay out in the countryside instead of in the cities. We cannot stress enough how much more value you receive when you avoid the cities - especially the tourist centers such as Rome, Florence, Milan and Venice. Of course stay right in the heart of town if you are not watching your budget, but if you are trying to squeeze the greatest value from your lire, choose hotels in the countryside and take side trips to visit the pricey tourist cities.


## HOTELS - RESERVATIONS

People frequently ask, "Do I need a hotel reservation?" The answer really depends on how flexible you want to be, how tight your time schedule is, which season you are travelling, and how disappointed you would be if your first choice is unavailable.

It is not unusual for the major tourist cities to be completely sold out during the peak season of June through September. Just as this guide was being written, a client wanted assistance with a hotel in Florence. Although we began six weeks in advance it took two days of phone calls contacting at least thirty hotels before we finally found a hotel - in the suburbs. So be forewarned. Hotel space in Rome, Florence and Venice is really at a premium and unless you don't mind taking your chances on a last-minute cancellation or staying on the outskirts of town, make a reservation. Space in the countryside is a little easier. However, if you have your heart set on some special little inn, you certainly should reserve as soon as your travel dates are firm. Reservations are confining. Most hotels will want a deposit to hold your room and frequently refunds are difficult should you change your plans - especially at the last minute. So it is a double bind: making reservations locks you into a solid framework, but without reservations you might be stuck with accommodations you do not like. During the height of the tourist season, some small hotels will only accept reservations for a minimum of three or more nights. However, do not give up because almost all of the hotels which have this policy will take a last-minute booking for a shorter period of time if you call along the way and there is space.   For those who like the security blanket of each night preplanned so that once you leave home you do not have to worry about where to rest your head, there are several options for making reservations which we have listed below.

*TRAVEL AGENT:*   A travel agent can be of great assistance - particularly if your own time is valuable.   A knowledgeable agent can handle all of the details of your holiday and "tie" it all together for you in a neat little package including hotel reservations, airline tickets, boat tickets, train reservations, ferry schedules, theater tickets, etc.   For your airline tickets there will be no service fee, but most travel agencies make a charge for their other services.   The best advice is to talk with your local agent.   Be frank about how much you want to spend and ask exactly what he can do for you and what the charges will be.   Although the travel agency in your town might not be familiar with all the little places in this guide, since many are so tiny that they appear in no other major sources, loan them your book - it is written as a guide for travel agents as well as for individual travellers.

*LETTER:*   If you start early, you can write to the hotels directly for your reservations.   There are certainly many benefits to this in that you can be specific as to your exact preferences.   The important point is to be brief in your request.   Clearly state the following: number of people in your party; how many rooms you desire; whether you want a private bathroom; date of arrival and date of departure; ask rate per night; and ask deposit needed.   When you receive a reply then send the deposit requested and ask for a receipt.   Note: when corresponding with Italy be sure to spell out the month.   Do not use numbers since in Europe they reverse our system - such as 6/9 means September 6, not June 9.

Mail to Italy is slow - allow about six weeks for an answer.   Although most hotels can understand a letter written in English, on page 227 we have provided a reservation request letter written in Italian with an English translation.   You can use this as a sample letter or photocopy it and use it for your actual request letters.

*TELEPHONE:* Our preference in making reservations is to call direct. The cost is minimal if you direct dial and you can have your answer immediately. If space is not available, you can then decide on an alternate. Ask your local operator about the best time to call for the lowest rates. Also consider the time change and what time it is in Italy so that you can call during their business day. Basically, the system is to dial 011 (the international code) 39 (Italy code). Compose these five numbers then dial the city code and the hotel telephone number which appears under the hotel listings.

*TELEX:* If you have access to a telex machine, this is another efficient way to reach a hotel. When a hotel has a telex we have included the number in the hotel listings. Again, be sure to be specific as to your arrival and departure dates, number in your party, and what type of room you want. And, of course, be sure to include your telex number for their response.

*U.S.REPRESENTATIVE:* Some hotels have a United States representative through whom reservations can be made. Many of these representatives have a toll free telephone number for your convenience. This is an extremely convenient and efficient way to secure a reservation. However, you might find it less expensive to make the reservation yourself since sometimes a representative makes a charge for his service, reserves only the more expensive rooms, or quotes a higher price to protect himself against currency fluctuations and administrative costs. Futhermore, usually only the larger or more expensive hotels can afford the luxury of a representative in the United States. Nevertheless, if you understand that it might cost you more, contacting the local hotel representative is an excellent method of making a reservation. We have listed in the hotel description section of this guide under each hotel those which have a United States representative and their telephone number.

# INFORMATION

If you have questions not answered in this guide or need special guidance for a particular destination, the Italian Government Travel Offices can asssit you:

*Italian Government Travel Office*
*630 Fifth Ave, Suite 1565, New York, NY 10111*
*telephone: (212) 245-4822*

*Italian Government Travel Office*
*360 Post Street, San Francisco, CA 94108*
*telephone: (415) 392-6206*

*Italian Government Travel Office*
*500 North Michigan Avenue, Chicago, IL 60611*
*telephone: (312) 644-0990*

*Italian Government Travel Office*
*3 Place Ville Marie, Montreal, Quebec, Canada*
*telephone: (514) 866-7667*


# ITINERARIES

In the first section of this guide you should be able to find an itinerary, or section of an itinerary, that can be easily custom tailored to fit your exact time frame and suit your own particular interests.  If your time is limited, you could certainly follow just a segment of an itinerary.  In the itineraries we have not specified numbers of nights at each destination, since to do so seemed much too confining.  Again, personality dictates what is best for a particular situation.  Some travellers like to see as much as possible in a short period of time and do not mind rising with the birds each morning to begin a new adventure.  For others, just the thought of packing and unpacking each night makes them shudder in horror and they would never stop for less than three or four nights at any one destination. A third type of tourist doesn't like to travel at all: the destination is the focus and he will use this guide to find the "perfect" resort from which he will never wander except for daytime excursions. So, once again, use this guide as a reference from which to plan your very own personalized trip.

Please note that although a hotel is suggested for each destination in an itinerary, the hotel is just that - a *SUGGESTION*. Perhaps the hotel seems over your budget, or too fancy, or too simple. Or just not "you". If this is the case just look in the back of the book and choose an alternate.

## MAPS

With each itinerary there is a map showing the routing and suggesting places of interest along the way. These are an artist's renderings and are not intended to replace a good commercial map. To supplement our generalized routings you will need a set of detailed maps which will indicate all of the highway numbers, expressways, alternate little roads, expressway access points, exact mileages, etc. Our suggestion would be to purchase a comprehensive selection of both city maps and regional maps before your departure, and with a highlight pen mark your own "personalized" itinerary and pinpoint your city hotels. If you live in a metropolitan area you should have no problem buying maps in a travel bookstore or else your local bookstore should be able to place a special order. Our personal preference for Italy are the *HALLWAG* maps. They make two maps, Southern Italy and Northern Italy, each of which comes with a small index booklet to help you find the towns you are seeking. Almost every town in our guide can be found on the Hallwag maps.

In this book, before the hotel description section, is a map of Italy showing all of the towns in which hotels are recommended. On this map each of the towns is marked with a number indicating its location. These numbers flow geographically across the map to aid you in finding alternate hotels should your first choice be unavailable.


## SECURITY WHILE TRAVELLING

The Italians make wonderful hosts. They are friendly, outgoing, gregarious and merry - no one is a "stranger". In fact, it seems every Italian has a brother or cousin in the United States, and so the warmth of camaraderie is further enhanced. In spite of the overall graciousness of the Italians, there are a few "misfits" who unfortunately have instilled in many tourists the idea that theft is rampant in Italy. True, I have heard stories about purses being snatched and cars pilfered - the same as anywhere in the world today. I have never had the impression that thieves were lurking around every corner, nor have I had anything stolen in Italy. Nevertheless, be cautious. Watch your purse. Don't let your wallet stand out like a red light in your back pocket. Lock your valuables in the hotel vault. Use travellers' checks. Don't leave valuables temptingly exposed in your car. In other words, use common sense. By following these simple rules you will avoid any unfortunate incidents that could tarnish the perfection of your holiday.


## SHOPPING

Italy is a shopper's paradise. Not only are the stores brimming with tempting merchandise, but their displays are beautiful, from the tiniest fruit market to the most chic boutique. Each area has its "specialty". In Venice items made from blown glass and handmade lace are very popular. Milan is famous for its clothing and silkwear (gorgeous scarves, ties and blouses). Florence is a paradise for leather goods (purses, shoes, wallets, gloves, suitcases) and also for gold jewelry (you can buy gold jewelry by weight). Rome is a fashion center where you can stroll the pedestrian shopping streets browsing in some of the world's most beautiful, sophisticated shops where you can buy the lastest designer creations and, of course, religious items are available, especially near St Peter's Cathedral. Naples and the surrounding regions (Capri, Ravello, Positano) offer delightful coral jewelry and also a wonderful selection of ceramics.

## TRANSPORTATION

*TRAINS:* Italy has an excellent network of trains. The major express trains are usually a quick, reliable way to whip between the major cities. In contrast, the local trains stop at every little town, take much longer, and are frequently delayed. Each train station is well organized. There is almost always an information desk where someone who speaks English will answer any questions and advise you as to the best schedules. There is another counter where you purchase your tickets. Still a third counter is where seat reservations are made. If you can possibly plan ahead, I strongly recommend purchasing your train tickets in advance since it quite time consuming to stand in two lines at each train station, only to find - particularly in summer - that the train you want is already sold out. You can purchase open tickets in the United States; however, when it is a local train, it is not always possible to purchase in advance your seat reservations. When this is the case, go ahead and buy the open tickets and then you can either buy your seat reservations locally, or else pay the concierge at your hotel to handle this transaction for you.

The very popular Eurail Pass is valid in Italy. This is a pass which allows unlimited travel on most trains throughout Europe. However, if you are going to travel only in Italy, then you might want to purchase instead one of the Italian Rail passes which are issued for either 8, 15, 21, or 30 days. You can choose either first or second class passes. These passes can be purchased through your travel agent or through the Italian State Railways in New York.

Another note on trains - in the summer when rail traffic is very heavy, unless you make dining car reservations in advance you might not be able to have the fun of eating your meal en route. If you have not made these reservations, as soon as you board the train, zip down to the dining car and ask to reserve a table.

*BOATS:* Italy has gorgeous islands dotting her shorelines, a glorious string of lakes gracing her mountains to the north, and romantic canals in Venice. Luckily Italy's boat system is excellent - enabling the tourist maximum enjoyment of some of Italy's most stunning destinations.

All of Italy's islands are linked to the mainland and serviced frequently by a wonderful maritime network. The many outlying islands often have overnight ferries which even offer sleeping accommodations and facilities for cars. The closer islands usually have a choice of conveyances - the hydrofoil which zips quickly across the water, or the regular ferry which is slower, but less expensive. The lakes too have an excellent system of boats. In fact, one of the highlights of travelling in Italy is to explore her glorious lakes by hopping on one of the ferry boats which glide romantically between the little villages clustered along the shoreline. Again, there is usually a choice of either the hydrofoil which darts between the hamlets, or the ferry which glides leisurely across the water and usually offers beverage and food service on board. The boat schedules are posted at each pier, or you can request a timetable from the Italian tourist office. One note: these little boats are punctual, to the minute, so be right at the pier with your ticket in hand so you can jump on board during the brief interlude that the boat huddles at the shore. If at all possible, squeeze in a short boat excursion while in Italy. It is a treat you will remember and it will enhance your trip.


## WEATHER

Italy is blessed with lovely weather. However, unless you are a ski enthusiast following the promise of what the majestic mountains have to offer in the winter, or must travel in summer due to school holidays, I highly recommend travelling in spring or fall. Travel at either of these times has two dramatic advantages: you miss the rush of the summer tourist season when all of Italy is packed, and you are most likely to have beautiful weather. In spring the meadows are painted with wildflowers and in fall the forests are a riot of color as the trees ready for winter.

Summer can be very hot, especially in the cities, and many hotels are not air conditioned. When they are, an additional charge is frequently included on the bill.

# WHAT TO WEAR

During the day informal wear is most appropriate including comfortable slacks for women.   In the evening, if you are at a sidewalk cafe or a simple pizzaria, women do not need to dress up nor men to wear coats and ties.   However, Italy   does have some elegant restaurants where definitely a dress and coat and tie are the proper wear.   I think a basic principle is to dress as you would in any city at home. There are perhaps a few special situations: the churches are still very conservative and shorts are definitely inappropriate.   In fact, some of the cathedrals still insist that women have their arms covered.   It is rare that a scarf on the head is required, but to wear one is a respectful gesture.

The "layered" effect is ideal for Italy.   Because Italy's climate runs the gamut from always cool in the mountains to frequently very hot in the south, the most efficient wardrobe is one where light blouses and shirts can be "reinforced" by layers of sweaters which can be added or peeled off as the day demands.

# Italian Highlights
## by Train & Boat

Riva

Lake Garda

MILANO  SIRMIONE  VERONA

Desenzano  Padua  VENICE

FLORENCE

ROME

Naples  Pompeii

CAPRI  SORRENTO

◉ OVERNIGHT STOPS

# Italian Highlights by Train & Boat

This itinerary can be journeyed easily by car; however, just the thought of taking an automobile onto an Italian expressway intimidates some of the bravest breed of tourist. I must admit that the Italians love cars and enjoy driving fast: it would seem that many are practicing for the Grand Prix. But an aversion to driving does not mean that your only alternative is a "package" tour. Italy can be seen splendidly by train and boat. This is a glorious way to travel and has many advantages such as: no one needs to watch the road instead of the scenery; family crises that occur when the map reader fails to notice the vital turnoff sign until it has zipped past can be avoided; a bottle of wine can be savored with lunch; and everyone arrives rested and ready to enjoy the sights. But maybe the best advantage of all is that while using local transportation you will make friends. Perhaps there will be just a smile at first, then maybe the sharing of a piece of fruit, or, later, the admiration of each other's family photographs. Somehow barriers break down on a long journey and the universal warmth of friendliness - at which the Italians are masters - spans the language barriers.

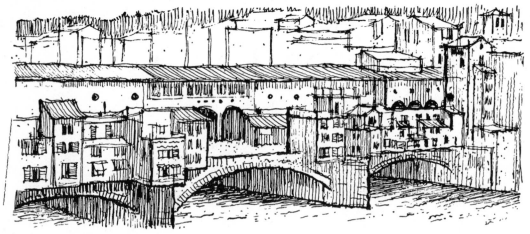

This itinerary covers some of the most famous destinations within Italy. For a short holiday it is impossible to include all the places of interest, but following this pathway will easily provide you with a glimpse of some of the highlights of Italy and will hopefully tempt you to return quickly to delve more deeply into the wonders that Italy has to offer. This itinerary is woven around towns that are conveniently linked by public transportation. Of course, if your time is extremely limited, this itinerary lends itself well to segmentation. If you cannot travel with us all the way, then choose what fits into your schedule and what most appeals to you personally. No matter what portion you include, you will be treated to a delightful holiday.

In the following itinerary approximate train and boat times have been included. Please note that these are given only as a reference to show you how the pieces of this itinerary tie together. Schedules are constantly changing, so these must be verified. Also, many boats and some trains are seasonal, so be very meticulous in making your plans.

## ORIGINATING CITY          MILAN

This highlight tour begins in MILAN, a most convenient city since it is the hub of airline flights from throughout Europe, plus is blessed with non-stop air service from the United States. Also, Milan is strategically located for trains arriving from all over Europe. Into her busy station trains come rushing via the Gotthard, Simplon and Bernina passes. However, it is not her location alone which makes Milan an ideal starting point. Although frequently bypassed as an enormous industrial city, Milan has at her core a truly charming metropolis which incorporates delights to please all tastes: some of the best shopping in Italy gorgeously displayed in glass-domed arcades, superb medieval squares snuggled unexpectedly within her boundaries, dazzling cathedrals, superb museums, gourmet restaurants, and, of course, La Scala - one of the world's most famous opera houses.

12:00 noon  depart Milan by train
 1:12 PM     arrive Desenzano

NOTE: This train usually departs from the Milan Central station, but sometimes the trains depart instead from the Porto Garibaldi station, so it is vital that schedules be checked very carefully.

When the train arrives in the ancient port of Desenzano, you can take a cab to the pier where the hydrofoils, steamers and buses leave for Sirmione. However, although more expensive, taking a cab directly to Sirmione (only about 6 miles away) is a splurge but also it is really the most convenient means of transportation since you can be taken directly to your hotel.

SIRMIONE is a walled medieval village fabulously located on a tiny peninsula jutting out into Lake Garda - actually almost an island because you first drive along a narrow thread of land and then magically enter Sirmione across the moat through the medieval gates!  Unless you are one of the lucky ones with a hotel for the night, you will not be allowed to enter by car since pedestrians only are allowed through the entrance.   But with hotel reservations, you can stop at the information office near the entrance and be given a pass to enter by car.

There are several hotels in the heart of Sirmione but the most glamorous choice, the VILLA CORTINE PALACE HOTEL, is located in a gorgeous park on the outskirts of town.   The entrance is absolutely "Hollywood".   You must ring a bell at the impressive gates which then slowly swing open allowing you to wind your way up through the truly beautiful park to the hotel which crowns the small hill. Previously, this was a sumptuous private villa.   Now a new wing has been built which doubles the original size.   Although the newer wing looks from the outside a bit sterile, the rooms are delightful and most have better views than those in the old section.  Demi-pension (breakfast and dinner) are required if you are staying at the Villa Cortine Palace.   In addition, reservations are usually taken only for stays of at least three nights. But neither should prove a problem - you will never want to leave such a delightful setting.

*Villa Cortine Palace*
*Sirmione*

From the Villa Cortine Palace Hotel you can easily walk to the wharf in the middle of town and study the boat schedule in order to make the delightful decision of which boat you want to take for your day's excursion.   You can either glide around the lake all day and have a snack on board, or you can get off in some small jewel of a town and enjoy lunch at a lakefront cafe.   There is also a small train, similar to those we have in some of our parks, which shuttles back and forth to the tip of the peninsula, so that those who prefer riding to walking can visit the small church and the Roman ruins.

There are trains almost every hour that cover the half-hour journey between Desenzano and Verona.   But if it is a beautiful day it might be much more fun to incorporate some sightseeing into your transportation and take a boat and bus instead. If so, the following gives an idea of how this can be done.

9:50  AM depart Sirmione by ferry
1:25   PM arrive Riva

You can have lunch on board the ferry or else you can wait until you reach the medieval town of RIVA, located on the northern shore of Lake Garda.   The terrace overlooking the lake at the Hotel Sole, located just across from where the ferry docks, provides a serene luncheon setting.   The ancient section of Riva is very small, so it will not take long to stroll the small square before you take one of the buses.   These leave fifteen times a day in summer for the ride along the eastern shore of the lake and then go on to Verona.

When you arrive in VERONA you will be delighted.   This is a town all too frequently bypassed, but what a prize.   The city is oozing with medieval charm and proudly boasts one of the most marvelous Roman amphitheaters in Italy - and that is saying a lot!   Luckily, Verona has several excellent hotels to complement her marvelous sights.   A delightful choice would be the HOTEL DUE TORRI.   It is strategically situated for walking, and offers much more than just location.   One of the fun and unique attributes of the hotel is the decor of its bedrooms: they all vary, each is individually decorated with its own personality and own period of furniture. If the hotel is not full, there is a clever slide presentation in the lobby where you can choose from the picture the bedroom which most suits your fancy.   Even if you are not able to pick your favorite style, you will enjoy the quality of decor: each of the bedrooms is furnished in genuine antiques, usually quite ornate and elegant, mostly from the 19th century.

*Hotel due Torri*
*Verona*

## DESTINATION III　　　VENICE　　HOTEL GRITTI PALACE

When you are ready to leave Verona, there is frequent train service to Venice so the following is just a suggestion.

2:20 PM depart Verona by train
3:50 PM arrive Venice, Santa Lucia station

As you come out of the front door of the train station you will find that the station is directly on the Grand Canal and that it is a few short steps down to where one boards a boat to take you to your hotel.　The Vaporetto is the most popular means of transportation and is very inexpensive.　This is like a "boat bus" which constantly shuttles back and forth from the train station to St Mark's Square.　The Number Two bus makes only major stops while the Number One bus pauses at every stop to exchange passengers.　Much more expensive, but a little faster, is the Motoscafo which is like a taxi and will take you wherever you want to go provided there is a motor boat dock. The Gondolas are much slower and even more expensive. (I would save my gondola ride for a more romantic interlude than a train connection.)

VENICE has many wonderful hotels in every price range. For this itinerary, perhaps the best is the GRITTI PALACE, a former home of the immensely wealthy Doge Andrea Gritti. And, indeed, you can believe it as you arrive in style at the hotel's dock on the Grand Canal and descend in grandeur onto the red carpet, past the diners enjoying a snack on the deck, and into the beautiful lobby. If price is of no matter, go all the way and request a room overlooking the canal.

*Hotel Gritti Palace*
*Venice*

Venice has so many sights; marvelous restaurants, beautiful boutiques, and fascinating little alleyways to explore, that you could happily stay for weeks. Of course, you will want to savor all the ambiance of St Mark's Square and visit the

Doges' Palace. See the Clock Tower whose huge bronze figures bang out the hours with massive hammers. Wander through the museums. Go either on your own or on a tour to the three islands of MURANO (famous for its hand-blown glass), BURANO (famous for its colorfully painted fishermen's cottages and the making of lace), and TORCELLO (once an important city but now just a small village with only its lovely large church to remind one of its past glories). A real bargain is to board the Vaporetto and enjoy the many wonderful palaces bordering the Grand Canal. My favorite recommendation in Venice is wandering - just anywhere - exploring the maze of twisting canals and criss-crossing back and forth over some of the 400 toy-like bridges.

Another outing you will certainly enjoy is to take the Il Burchiello, named for a famous 17th-century Venetian boat, which leaves Tuesdays, Thursdays and Saturdays at about 9:20AM from Pontile Giarinetti pier at St Mark's Square and travels the network of rivers and canals linking Venice and Padua. (The schedule might change, so verify.) This little boat, with an English speaking guide on board, stops at several of the exquisite palaces en route. Lunch is served and there is time for sightseeing in Padua before returning to Venice by bus. This is a delightful excursion.

## DESTINATION IV          FLORENCE          LUNGARNO HOTEL

There are several direct trains each day from Venice to Florence: however, in summer, space is at a real premium, so be sure to reserve a seat in advance. Some of the express trains must have prior seat reservations and will require a supplemental fee. NOTE: If you want to dine on the train, it is necessary, during the busy season, to make reservations in advance when you buy your ticket.

12:00 noon depart Venice, Santa Lucia station (train "Marco Polo")
 3:08 PM  arrive Florence

In FLORENCE, stay perhaps at the LUNGARNO HOTEL, which rises directly from the banks of the Arno very near the Ponte Vecchio. The Lungarno is not an "old-world" hotel, but rather a modern, very tastefully decorated, charming hotel perched directly on the Arno only steps from the heart of Florence. Although new, the Lungarno happily qualifies without too much stretch of the imagination for our inn series because it incorporates into its construction a 13th-century tower in which there are some romantic rooms. However, my preference would be a room in the front overlooking the river - a few even have balconies for those lucky travellers who book well in advance.

*Lungarno Hotel*
*Florence*

Be generous with your time and do not rush Florence - there is too much to see. You must, of course, pay a visit to Michelangelo's David in the Accademia (located just off the Piazza San Marco), and you must not miss the fantastic museums and cathedrals - the world will probably never again see a city which has produced so much artistic genius. Travellers best appreciate Florence when they are simply roaming. Wander through the streets and poke into small boutiques. Stop in churches which catch your eye - they all abound with masterpieces. Sit to enjoy a cappuchino in one of the little sidewalk cafes and "people watch". Stroll through the piazzas and watch some of the artists at work - many of them incredibly clever - as they paint portraits and do sculptures for a small fee. End your day by finding the perfect small restaurant for a delicious pasta made by mama in the back kitchen.

## DESTINATION V ROME HOTEL FORUM

There is excellent train service from Florence to Rome. It is probably best to take one of the midday trains which will allow you to enjoy lunch as you soak in the beauty of the Tuscany hills flowing by your window. Remember that you will need both seat and dining reservations.

11:41 AM depart Florence via train
 1:48 PM arrive Rome, Termini station

As the train pulls into the enormous city of ROME, you will feel overwhelmed by its size, but once you settle into the FORUM and go up to the delightful rooftop terrace for a panoramic view of the city, you will be highly motivated to begin the exploration of this fabulous city of archaeological wonders. Note: if you do choose the Forum, we recommend splurging and requesting one of the larger guest rooms.

Rome is bursting with a wealth of fantastic museums, ancient monuments, spectacular cathedrals, gourmet restaurants, beautiful boutiques, colorful piazzas, whimsical fountains, inspiring statues, theater, opera...the city itself is a virtually a museum. One cannot possibly savor it all. Do get an excellent guidebook and decide what is top priority for your own special interests. If there are several in your party, then a private guide might be money well spent since he will custom tailor your sightseeing.   With a private guide you can squeeze much more quality sightseeing into a short period of time.

*Hotel Forum*
*Rome*

## DESTINATION VI    SORRENTO    GRAND HOTEL EXCELSIOR VITTORIA

One could spend weeks discovering the museum that is Rome, but if you have time to add a few more highlights before your return, try to include Sorrento and Capri. There is frequent train service from Rome to Naples and from there it is a short Aliscafi (hydrofoil) ride to Capri.  However, for the adventurous it is fun to include Pompeii and Sorrento en route.   Please be advised that this makes a long day of travel and takes some manipulating of schedules, but the rewards are great.

You will need an early start to accomplish a tour of Pompeii on your way to Sorrento, but this is a must.   How could you be so close to this intriguing city of the Romans which was frozen in time by the ashes of Vesuvius without a visit?

 9:00  AM depart Rome, Termini station
11:44  AM arrive Pompeii, Main station

You ARRIVE in POMPEII at the main station, but you will DEPART from Pompeii at the Villa d. Misteri station, located just across from the main entrance to the archaeological site.   Since you will need to store your baggage while you sightsee, I suggest taking a cab from the Main station to the Villa d. Misteri station and checking your suitcases, then you can just walk across the street to the main gate of Pompeii.   There is a nice terrace restaurant by the entrance and also a cafe inside.   If you want to do your own touring, you can buy an excellent guidebook in English from a stall, or else you can negotiate with one of the licensed guides for a personal tour.   You may have heard that the earthquake of 1980 destroyed much of Pompeii.   It is true that many of the sites were damaged and some are still under reconstruction, but do not worry, there is still enough to keep you busy for hours. An aura of mystery lingers in the air as you wander the streets of Pompeii.   All are touched by this ancient city which, in one day, was frozen for all time.

As you explore Pompeii, there is no need to watch your clock because there is a fun, narrow gauge train departing from the Pompeii Villa d. Misteri station about every twenty minutes for the half-hour scenic journey to Sorrento.

When you arrive in SORRENTO, stay at the GRAND HOTEL EXCELSIOR VITTORIA, a romantic old villa at the center of town in a prime cliff location overlooking the harbor.   The hotel's once perfect grandeur is perhaps a bit faded, but as you sit on the terrace in the evening and watch the sun turning the bay into shades of red and gold, the atmosphere is perfection.   There is also a pool for relaxing and sunning.   Definitely ask for a deluxe room with a view.

*Grand Hotel Excelsior Vittoria*
*Sorrento*

## DESTINATION VII          CAPRI          GRAND HOTEL QUISISANA

When it is time to leave Sorrento there is excellent service by either hydrofoil or ferry to Capri.  Perhaps the following schedule will give you a suggestion:

5:45 PM depart Sorrento by hydrofoil
6:30 PM arrive Capri

Your hydrofoil will arrive at the Marina Grande where you will find major hotel representatives on the pier.  They will relieve you of your luggage and take it directly to your room.  You can then walk over to take either a mini-bus or the funicular to the main town of CAPRI.

There are many small hotels on Capri but, if you want to splurge, a deluxe hotel choice is the GRAND HOTEL QUISISANA. A larger hotel than most recommended in this guide, it is an oasis at the heart of Capri where you can retreat to a haven during the heat of the day and relax by the beautiful pool. During the day, the island is swarming with tourists who come on day tours. I used to think that in the evening the activity subsided. This isn't so! The tour groups leave at dusk but from the deluxe villas and fancy hotels a new group emerges in their chic clothes and fancy jewelry to stroll the streets - there both to see and be seen.

*Grand Hotel Quisisana*
*Capri*

Capri has many wonders. The most famous is its submerged cave, the BLUE GROTTO, which can be reached by boat when the seas are calm. Large boats begin leaving the harbor every morning at 9:00 AM for the short ride to the entrance to the Blue Grotto, where you are transferred into tiny rowboats. The excursion is an adventure in itself. As your little boat approaches the tiny cave opening it seems impossible there will be adequate room, but suddenly the sea surges forward and in you squeeze. Like magic you see it - the mysterious stunning blue light reflecting from some hidden source which illuminates the grotto.

Capri is also a marvelous island for walking. As you stroll the trails, all your senses will be treated by the fragrant flowers, the gorgeous vistas of the brilliant blue waters and the sound of birds luring you ever onward. There are many spectacular walks. Follow the trail winding down the cliffs to the small harbor on the opposite side called MARINA PICCOLA. There are lovely views of the shimmering aqua waters as you make your way to the small beach where you can enjoy a swim before your return. Instead of walking back up the hill, take the little bus which will deliver you quickly back to the main square.

Another absolutely spectacular walk - although a long one of at least 45 minutes each way - is to Emperor Tiberius's palace, perched high on the cliffs on the western tip of the island. From there the view is incredible! You can have an overview of the whole island and watch the ferries shuttling back and forth to the mainland. This spot among the ruins makes the perfect picnic place, so pack a feast of famous Italian salami, cold pasta salad and crisp, fruity Soave wines, and soak in the view.

A much shorter walk, but one equally as beautiful, is to the Cannone Belvedere. This tiny walkway guides you near delightful private villas hidden behind high walls (you can get glimpses through the gates) and on to a promontory overlooking the sea.

When the real world calls and you must leave Capri, there is frequent ferry or hydrofoil service back to Naples. From there, you can take either a train to Rome or a plane to your next destination.

# Mountain &
# Lake Adventures

SWITZERLAND

AUSTRIA

Aosta
Chiavenna
MERANO
Bolzano
Bressanone
CORTINA
I PESCATORI
BELLAGIO
OBEREGGEN
Belluno
CHAMPOLUC
Stresa
Trent
ASOLO
Maser
Bergamo
GARDONE
Marostica
FRANCE
Turin
Milan
Sirmione
VENICE

Genoa
Bologna

Florence

◉ OVERNIGHT STOPS

37

# Mountain & Lake Adventures

For the traveller who wants to combine the magic of seeing some of the world's most splendid mountains with the joy of visiting Italy's gorgeous northern lakes, this itinerary will be ideal. Contrasts will heighten the impact of visual delights as you meander across northern Italy through lovely mountain passes, through lush green meadows laced with wildflowers, beneath giant mountains piercing the sky with their jagged granite peaks, and bordering lazy blue lakes whose steep shorelines are decorated with endearing little Italian villages wrapped in misty cloaks of wonderful siennas and ochres. What a glorious holiday to wind across northern Italy enjoying some of her most beautiful landscapes. This itinerary can delightfully stand alone. However, it is also perfect for the traveller arriving or departing from neighboring countries. We have carefully shown detours for the tourist who will be leaving or entering from Austria, Switzerland, or France. All too often the tourist thinks he has "finished" Italy when his tour ends in Venice and he too quickly rushes north into Austria or Switzerland. What a waste. A very promising picturesque region still remains. Please try to linger to enjoy some of the mountains and lakes which truly are some of Italy's greatest natural artistic treasures.

ORIGINATING CITY          VENICE

═══════════════════════════════════════════════════════════════

This itinerary begins in VENICE, one of the most romantic cities in the world. Her maze of waterways are criss-crossed by storybook little bridges and shadowed by majestic palaces whose soft hues warmly reflect in the shimmering water.   Here black gondolas quietly glide through the minute canals as the gondolier in his red and white striped shirt softly serenades his romantic passengers with an operatic selection.   Venice is not a traditional city, rather an archipelago of 117 islands "glued" together by 400 bridges.


DESTINATION I          ASOLO          HOTEL VILLA CIPRIANI

═══════════════════════════════════════════════════════════════

You need not rush your departure this morning.   Venice is a city that should be enjoyed slowly and since your journey today is short, you can certainly have the luxury of a last leisurely breakfast before embarking on your next adventure.

Since all the "streets" in Venice are liquid, you will need to take a boat to your car. It will probably be at the Piazzale Roma where most of the car rental companies are located: in addition it is also where there are overnight car parks for storing your car if you drive into Venice.   The choice of conveyance will depend upon your budget and your inclination.   The Vaporetto is the most reasonable.   Similar to a river bus, the Vaporetto leaves regularly from St Mark's Square for the approximately half-hour ride to the Piazzale Roma.   The Vaporetto Number One stops at most of the little docks along the route whereas Vaporetto Number Two is an express boat which stops at only a few major points.   The Motoscafi are motorboats which duck through the back canals and usually take about fifteen minutes to the Piazzale Roma.   The Motoscafi are like private cabs and are much more expensive than the "bus", but can be very convenient, especially if your hotel has a private motor boat landing. The most deluxe mode of transportation is by private Gondola: however, these are very expensive and usually take about an hour to reach the Piazzale Roma.

Once you have retrieved your car from the parking garage or have finished the paper work for your car rental, head north from Venice toward TREVISO which requires about an hour's drive. If time allows, try to stop here. Stroll through this picturesque city spider-webbed with canals and surrounded by 15th-century ramparts. Perhaps have a cup of coffee or a bite of lunch before heading north toward Asolo. Treviso is famous for its arcaded streets, churches lavishly decorated with frescoes, and many delightfully painted houses. You might want to climb the ramparts for a view of the Alps beckoning you on. From Treviso it is approximately another hour to Asolo. However, just a few miles before you reach Asolo you should see signs for the town of MASER where the marvelous VILLA DI MASER (some of your books might use the name of VILLA BARARO) is located. This is a splendid villa designed by Palladio and fabulously decorated with frescoes by Paolo Veronese. This elegant villa has erratic days and hours when it is open to the public - usually in late afternoons on Tuesdays, Saturdays and Sundays. However, it is only about one mile out of your way, so well worth a detour to investigate. There is also a very interesting museum of old carriages and antique cars at Villa di Maser.

Your prize tonight is ASOLO. Asolo is an absolute delight. It is a gem of a small medieval village snuggled on the side of a hill with lovely views of the countryside. As you drive toward it the terrain does not seem to hold much promise - just modern towns and industry - but then the signs point to Asolo and the road winds up a lovely hillside and into the tiny village which encompasses a delightful combination of a "real" town with its gorgeous fruit stands, candy shops, colorful little grocery store, etc. for those lucky few who live in Asolo; plus, gorgeous shops with beautiful merchandise for the tourist. Of course a castle adorns the hill above the village - mostly in ruins but setting the proper stage. Naturally, there is a wonderful cathedral dominating the square, just as it should. You will find all this plus vineyards and olive trees on the hillsides and the scent of roses in the air. No wonder Robert Browning fell in love with Asolo and chose it as his home. It might not be possible for all to live here, but you will have the marvelous option of the **VILLA CIPRIANI** which is a superb villa (once the home of Robert Browning) where you too can pretend that Asolo is yours. Sit on the lovely terrace and watch the soft lights paint the distant villa-dotted hills in mellow shades of gold.

*Hotel Villa Cipriani*
*Asolo*

## DESTINATION II          CORTINA          HOTEL MENARDI

There are a couple of towns which are worth seeing before leaving the Asolo area. If brandy holds a special interest for you, visit **BASSANO DEL GRAPPA**, an old town famous for its production of grappa (or brandy). The town is also a pottery center. However, it is rather large, and, in my estimation, much less interesting than a tiny town just a few miles farther on, MAROSTICA.   If you are in this area in September, I would suggest that you check on dates and consider a stop in Marostica because on the first Sunday in September - in alternate years - the central square is transformed into a giant chess board and local citizens become the human chess pieces.   Even if it isn't the year of the chess game, Marostica is a cute little medieval town encircled by walls whose delightful little central square is surrounded by colorful buildings with a castle forming one side.   There is also a second castle guarding the town from the top of the hill.

As you head north into the Dolomites there are various routes to choose from. The major highway heads north through Feltre and Belluno and then on to Cortina. However, if the day is nice and your spirit of adventure is high, there is really nothing more fun than the "back roads" through the mountains.   The Michelin maps are a great aid in this respect because they mark in green various small roads which are particularly scenic, and as you head north you can experiment with these choices and your journey should take you through tiny hamlets and gorgeous mountain valleys far from the normal tourist path.

You might want to be loose and just choose your own little country inn in one of the lovely little valleys of the Dolomites, but if you are making reservations, I would suggest an overnight in CORTINA D'AMPEZZO.   This is not a little town.   In fact, it has grown into a large tourist center due to its excellent skiing facilities: however, the location is truly superb, with gigantic granite peaks ringing the town. In Cortina there are many hotels.   I prefer one with a history that dates back far before the skiing craze, the MENARDI.   According to the charming owner, Angelo Menardi, the inn was originally a peasant home - in his family for 150 years. Gradually the farmhouse became an inn giving shelter to those seeking a bed for the night - more often than not in the hay loft.   Times have changed and today the Menardi is a proper hotel where the guests sleep in beds with down comforters and all the guest rooms have private baths.   However, much of the original atmosphere remains, with marvelous antiques cleverly incorporated into the decor.   Great taste and personal warmth exude throughout.

*Hotel Menardi*
*Cortina*

Although the Menardi was originally a farmhouse, civilization has crept in and today the inn is located on the north side of Cortina directly on the main highway heading toward Toblach.

## DESTINATION III   VAL D'EGA - OBEREGGEN   HOTEL BEWALLERHOF

When it is time to leave Cortina for further mountain adventures you will be taking the Old Dolomite Road heading west from Cortina to Bolzano.   This historic pass was originally used by the merchants of Venice on their way to Germany.   Follow the highway S48 from Cortina which will take you over a windswept barren pass surrounded by towering granite peaks.   The road then drops into a valley before climbing again to conquer the Pordoi Pass and then down into the Fassa Valley. When you reach the town of Vigo di Fassa leave the road you are on and head west over the Carezza Pass. Along the way on your left you will pass Lake Carezza which, although small, is certainly worth a stop to savor this delightful green lake surrounded by mountain peaks. Soon after leaving Lake Carezza you arrive in the town of Nova Levante.

The route from Cortina to Nova Levante is well marked, but from this town on you will need to watch for the road signs. Just a few miles beyond Nova Levante you will come to a junction. At this intersection take the road to the left and, keeping to the left, follow the signs for EGA, EGGEN, OBEREGGEN, or SAN FLORIANO. In this part of Italy the town names are most confusing because each town is named both in Italian and also with the old Austrian name since before the first world war this section of Italy belonged to the Austrian Empire. So, Ega and Eggen are the same town, and Obereggen and San Floriano are the same town.

*Hotel Bewallerhof*
*Val D'Ega, Obereggen*

Your hotel, the HOTEL BEWALLERHOF, is located between these two tiny hamlets. It sounds complicated to find. It is. You will probably get lost along the way, after leaving Nova Levante, but just stop and ask directions and make certain you have a detailed map. (The best ones, which you will be able to find in Cortina, are the VERY detailed hiking path maps which also have the highways indicated.) If the weather is clear this route from Cortina to Obereggen will take you through some of the most glorious mountains in the world, and when you reach your final destination, you will find yourself in one of the really special "hideaways" in the world, the idyllic Hotel Bewallerhof.

Whereas your last hotel was in the bustling town of Cortina, the Bewallerhof is almost as isolated as a hotel can be. Leaving the town of Ega (or Eggen) you will soon see a sign on the left of the road reading "Bewallerhof". Turning left, you weave through a pine forest which then opens into a meadow crowned by an small hotel, built upon the site of an old farmhouse (this is still farming country with pastures and cows neaby adding to the country ambiance). The deck dominating the front of the hotel has a panoramic view which stretches for miles over grassy fields which sweep down to rows of mountains. Behind the hotel the granite peaks of the Dolomites rise dramatically in the sky forming a majestic natural backdrop.

For some tastes the Bewallerhof will be too isolated. For some personalities the hotel will be too simple. But you will definitely not be "roughing it ": all the rooms have private baths and the decor is simple but very inviting with light wooden furniture, plants, and lots of paneling. The emphasis is on the outdoors. What bliss to walk for miles in any direction surrounded by such beauty.

If you are a mountain enthusiast you might just decide to stay forever at the Hotel Bewallerhof, but when it is time to continue on, be consoled by the fact that there is another magnificent hotel awaiting at the end of your day's journey and a wonderful town to visit en route.

When you depart from Obereggen return to the main road, marked S241, and follow the splendid Val d'Ega (Ega Valley) as it weaves its way through a dramatic gorge.   The road joins the main expressway just north of Bolzano where I recommend taking the expressway north to BRESSANONE.   Try to time your stop at Bressanone for lunch because this small city has much to offer.   It is a walled medieval town ringed by mountains.   There is a charming little village square plus a river - lined on both banks by promenades - meandering through the center. Bressanone hides another treasure, the ELEFANT.   This inn is famous for its exquisite cuisine.   In its beautiful dining rooms only the freshest foods and wines are served - usually from the hotel's own farms and vineyards.   But the hotel also has an intriguing tale.   In the 16th century an elephant was being delivered to Maximilian of Austria as a special gift.   Well, it seems this "gift" grew weary of walking by the time it arrived in Bressanone and so was housed at the local inn - you guessed it - the Elefant.   The story alone merits a stop, but the joy is that the Elefant also retains so much character and serves such excellent food.

From Bressanone you can take the expressway north toward the Brenner Pass, soon leaving the expressway near Vipiteno to head southwest along a twisting road which maneuvers along the Monte Giovo Pass as it twists its way through the mountains and then drops down into the valley to follow the Passiria River which winds a path into Merano.

DETOUR NOTE: If your destination is Austria, then at Vipiteno continue north on the expressway for the short drive to the Brenner Pass leading into Austria.

In MERANO I suggest the CASTEL FREIBERG, an enchanting fairytale castle on a knoll of a hill dominating the countryside with its majesty. This fabulous castle has everything - setting, view, marvelous architecture, gourmet food, beautiful rooms, priceless antiques, pool, tennis, and friendly, professional management.

*Castel Freiberg*
*Merano*

## DESTINATION V        GARDONE RIVIERA        VILLA FIORDALISO

It is a short drive south from Merano to Bolzano where you will meet the freeway heading toward Trent which in the 16th century was the town where the Catholic council met to establish important articles of faith which emphasized the authority of the Catholic church.

*Hotel Villa Fiordaliso*
*Gardone Riviera*

Leave the freeway at Trent and head west toward the small but lovely green LAKE TOBLINO which is enhanced by a superb castle on its north shore where you can stop for lunch. From Toblino there is a beautiful country road lined with fruit trees and vineyards which heads directly south to Lake Garda, Italy's largest lake. On the northern shore of Lake Garda is the town of RIVA. Although the town has grown with the construction of modern facilities to accommodate the tourists, there is still a nucleus forming the Old Town of Riva near the harbor where you will find the Piazza III Novembre and the Tower of Apponale which dates from the 13th century.

Leaving Riva, take the road along the western shoreline. It is a kaleidoscope of vistas as the road weaves through 70 tunnels and over 56 bridges snaking its way along the cliffs. Each tunnel holds a new surprise as you emerge to view the lake from a fresh perspective. You pass through several small villages and a few minutes before arriving in GARDONE RIVIERA you will see a small, elegant, pink and white villa on the lefthand side of the road. There will be a sign indicating you have arrived at the VILLA FIORDALISO, and just beyond the villa, the road turns off into a parking area beneath the trees in a parklike area beside the hotel. The hotel's fame is as a luxurious restaurant, but luckily there are seven rooms for the overnight guest. In addition to having superb meals and a delightful lakefront location, the Villa Fiordaliso has a romantic history: this was once the romantic hideaway for Mussolini and his mistress, Claretta. Ask for one of the bedrooms overlooking the garden - not only will it be quieter, but you will also have a view of the lake.

The town of Gardone Riviera is an excellent choice for a lake interlude due to its central location which lends itself beautifully to exploring by hydrofoil or steamer the delightful villages which hug the shore of the lake. If you have the time, I would choose a different destination each day - perhaps planning to have a bite of lunch at an appealing little lakeside cafe. However, if you have time for only one adventure, I recommend taking a ferry or hydrofoil to the scenic town of SIRMIONE, a wonderful walled village at the south end of Lake Garda positioned at the end of a miniature peninsula which proudly pokes it head into the lake. During the summer this town is absolutely bursting with tourists: but you can certainly understand. This is another one of Italy's "stage setting" villages, almost too perfect to be true. If you take the ferry or hydrofoil to Sirmione your boat will dock in the center of the town and you can stroll through the little boutiques, perhaps have a bite of lunch at one of the beautiful terrace cafes overlooking the lake, and explore the tiny island-like village. Sirmione is definitely one of Europe's most picturesque villages.

In addition to the marvelous lake excursions, while at Gardone Riviera you might want to visit a museum nearby, the VITTORIALE, once the home of Gabriele D'Annunzio, the celebrated Italian poet. (For those of us who love stories of romance, D'Annunzio is also famous for his love affair with Eleanora Duse.)

It might be easier to leave the Villa Fiordaliso knowing that the GRAND HOTEL VILLA SERBELLONI on Lake Como awaits your arrival.  The Villa Serbolloni will be a nice contrast because although both are lakefront, the Villa Fiordaliso is intimate and tiny whereas the Villa Serbelloni is large and imposing.

On your way from your villa on Lake Garda to your villa on Lake Como, I highly suggest making one stop.  You will pass through a fabulous town which should not be missed, BERGAMO, only about an hour's drive west of Gardone Riviera.  As you approach Bergamo it will not look worth a stop -  but it is.  The shell of the city is deceiving because it hides a lovely kernel, the CITA ALTA, or high city.  The lower part of Bergamo is modern and pleasant, but the old medieval city snuggled on the top of the hill holds such treasures as the Piazza Vecchia, the Colleoni Chapel, and the Church of St Mary Major.  Should you want to time your stop in Bergamo with lunch, there are several excellent restaurants.  A delicious family style meal can be had at the Agnello d'Oro, a cozy, charming l7th-century inn in the Cita Alta.

From Bergamo it is a short drive on to BELLAGIO, a medieval port located at the tip of a peninsula dividing the lower section of Lake Como into two lakes, Lake Como on the west and Lake Lecco on the east. In this town with gates opening onto the main square is your hotel, the Grand Hotel Villa Serbelloni, a large imposing "old-world" style palace hotel offering everything you could wish for in a lakeside interlude - tennis, swimming pool, boat excursions, private beach, and more.  The Villa Serbelloni is very ornate, still retaining its glory of bygone days.  In fact the hotel is almost overwhelming with its soaring ceilings intricately painted, heavy chandeliers, and a fabulous sweeping staircase.  The setting of the Villa Serbelloni is superb and overshadows what might be perceived as a slightly "faded elegance" of the hotel's decor.

*Villa Serbelloni*
*Bellagio*

Just a few steps from the hotel lies charming, medieval Bellagio where you can meander through the village or walk to the pier for one of the boats which will take you to all corners of the lake. What a wonderful excursion. Lake Como is absolutely beautiful - especially the lower eastern branch of the lake called Lake Lecco where cliffs enclose the shorelines like gorgeous walls and give a fjord-like beauty to the area. There are numerous romantic steamers which glide in and out of the picturesque, softly hued little hamlets dotting the lake shore. You can settle onto a steamer equipped with bar and restaurant and from your armchair lazily enjoy the constantly changing, but always intriguing shoreline as the boat maneuvers in and out of the colorful little harbors, past elegant private villas, by postcard-pretty villages. From Bellagio you can also step on board one of the swift hydrofoils which will whisk you about the lake. Or, from Bellagio you can put your car right on the ferry to either Cadenabbia on the western shore of Lake Como or Varenna on the eastern shore of the lake. With Bellagio as a base there are several sightseeing possibilities. An excursion to visit the VILLA CARLOTTA, a fairytale-like 18th-century palace - worthy of the Prussian Princess Carlotta for whom it was named - is enjoyable. My suggestion would be to take the car ferry from Bellagio to Cadenabbia on the western shore. From there it is just a short drive along the beautiful tree lined Via del Paradiso to the Villa Carlotta which is encircled by its own gorgeous park of terraced gardens.

## DESTINATION VII    ISOLA DEI PESCATORI    HOTEL VERBANO

DETOUR NOTE: Should your plans call for ending your Italian sojourn and heading on into Switzerland this would be an excellent point to begin your journey. Head north along Lake Como and on to Chiavenna where you then turn east for the short drive (only about 6 miles) to the Swiss border. From there it is a lovely drive through the Engadine Valley to St Moritz.

Continuing on toward LAKE MAGGIORE, take advantage of the expressways to make your drive as easy as possible because there is usually heavy traffic in this part of Italy. It is best to head directly south from Bellagio to pick up the freeway in the direction of Milan. Keep on the bypass which skirts to the north of Milan and follow the freeway northwest to Lake Maggiore. When you reach the lake continue along the western shore to STRESA. It seems only suitable that for a "Mountain and Lake Adventure" one of your hotels should be located on an island in a lake - so we have chosen for you one of the Borromean Islands, ISOLA DEI PESCATORI (Fisherman's Island), located in Lake Maggiore. This is an enchanting little island with twisting, narrow alley-like streets and colorful fishermen's cottages. As the name implies, this is still an active fishing village. During the tourist season the island teems with people and the streets are lined with rather tacky souvenir shops, but it is hard to dull the charm of this quaint town.

*Hotel Verbano*
*Isola dei Pescatori*

This island can be reached by ferry from Stresa, Baveno, or Pallanza, but the most popular of these is Stresa from which there are frequent departures by boat to Isola dei Pescatori. Your hotel, the VERBANO, is definitely not a deluxe hotel. In fact, it would not be suitable for those who enjoy only fancy hotels because this is a small, very simple, very basic hotel. The lobby is quite plain. The bedrooms too are very simple. However, if you appreciate all kinds of hotels for the special attributes they have to offer, I think you will love the Verbano. It has a delightful terrace with dining tables set overlooking the lake; the bedrooms too have beautiful vistas and some even offer large patios. The food is delicious (the same cook for 28 years), and the service of the Zacchera family, who own and personally manage the Verbano, is warm and gracious.

This tiny archipelago consisting of Isola Bella (Beautiful Island), Isola dei Pescatori (Fisherman's Island), and Isola Madre (Mother Island) are world famous for their dramatic palaces and spectacular, fragrant gardens. How smug you will be to settle into your room then have a drink on the lovely terrace and watch the last of the tourists hustle onto the boat for shore, leaving you to enjoy the sunset.

## DESTINATION VIII          CHAMPOLUC          ANNA MARIA

DETOUR NOTE: Should your next destination be Zermatt, then it is time to leave Italy by heading north to Domodossolo. About 10 miles beyond Domodossolo you arrive at Iselle where you drive your car piggyback style onto the train and ride in your car as you zigzag through the fabulous Simplon Tunnel and emerge about 20 minutes later in Brig, Switzerland.

*Anna Maria*
*Champoluc*

From Verbano drive south to the main freeway and head west toward Turin. Before reaching Turin watch for the signs and take the branch of the expressway heading toward Aosta. When you come to Verres, leave the highway and take the small road north to CHAMPOLUC, an hour's drive. The road follows the Evancon River as it cuts its path through the mountains. At first the valley is quite steep and narrow and then opens up into wide meadows lazily stretching out on both sides of the river. In early summer the meadows are truly lovely, blanketed in brilliantly colored wild flowers.

Just before the road leaves Champoluc you will see a marker for the ANNA MARIA HOTEL. At this sign turn to the right and follow the road for a very short drive up the hill until you see the hotel. It is beautifully located amid the pine trees and has views in every direction of the spectacular mountains. The Anna Maria is a charming small chalet-style inn owned and managed by the gracious and efficient Anna Maria. The dining room is cozy and inviting with gay red checked curtains at the windows and rustic Alpine-style carved wooden chairs. The bedrooms, although small, all have private bathrooms and are most appealing with paneled walls and a country flavor.

When it is time to leave Champoluc you have two options if you want to travel into Switzerland. First you must drive back to the main expressway and head west. In about a half hour you will come to Aosta at which point you can leave the expressway for the road leading north to the San Bernardino tunnel and into Switzerland's Rhone Valley. Or, by continuing on the expressway west through the village of Courmayeur, you arrive at the Mont Blanc tunnel which delivers you briefly into France, but within a hour more to Geneva by a main highway. Of course, by taking the short drive to Milan you can easily "tie in" with another Italian holiday suggested in this guide.

*Mountain & Lake Adventures*

# Romantic Hilltowns of
# Tuscany & Umbria

FLORENCE

PANZANO
IN CHIANTI

Arezzo

San Gimignano• •Siena   •Cortona

Abbey of Monte   SINALUNGA   ASSISI
Oliveto Maggiore   •Perugia
         Pienza   Torgiano

                    Spoleto
Orvieto•           •Monteluco

    Todi•

•ROME

◉ OVERNIGHT STOPS

# Romantic Hilltowns of Tuscany & Umbria

Nothing could possibly surpass the exquisite beauty of the countryside near Florence in the spring. It is absolutely breathtaking. Actually, any time of the year, if you meander into the hilltowns south of Florence, all your senses will be rewarded with the splendors that this enchanting Italian countryside has to offer. Almost every hillock is crowned with a picture-perfect little walled village. The fields are brilliant with vibrant red poppies. The vineyards lace the fields in all their glory and promise. The dusky grey-green of the olive trees dresses the hillsides. Pine forests unexpectedly appear to highlight the landscape. As if this were not enough, this area conceals within her little villages and countryside retreats some of the finest small hotels in all the world. And if this is still not sufficient to tempt you away from the normal tourist route, be reminded that the food and wines are superb.

So, when you plan your trip to Italy, please allow time to treat yourself to a unique adventure. Save at least a few days to slip away from the cities and into the countryside. Perhaps you will not have time to follow this entire itinerary, but at least sneak in a few days in this magnificent area. You will be well rewarded with a wealth of memories which will linger long after you return home.

| ORIGINATING CITY | FLORENCE |
|---|---|

Your journey begins in FLORENCE. Allow enough time to savor this marvelous city but, if you are reluctant to leave, be consoled. There are magnificent treats in store for you in the delightful hilltowns which surround Florence. Great art was not confined within the city limits of Florence and you will see magnificent cathedrals and beautiful works of art throughout the neighboring areas. Yet the real treats in store for you are not only the masterpieces made by man, but also those made by God.

| DESTINATION I | ASSISI | HOTEL SUBASIO |
|---|---|---|

The traffic around Florence is difficult, so quickly find the expressway to Rome and follow it until you come to the turnoff for Arezzo, which is located about 6 miles east of the highway. You might want to bypass Arezzo. Although it is a medieval town with a rich history dating back to the Etruscan era, it is a large city and it is not as quaint as some of its smaller neighbors.

If you follow the main road south from Arezzo, you will soon arrive at CORTONA. This is a beautifully situated walled town climbing up a steep hillside covered with olive trees. Stop to enjoy the atmosphere of this medieval town with its crazy little twisting streets, jumble of small squares and colorful buildings. A mighty castle stands guard dramatically over this hillside town.

Leaving Cortona, continue south to Lake Trasimeno and follow the northern shore on to PERUGIA, a large medieval city encompassed by ramparts. An important Umbrian city since Etruscan days, the heart of the old city is the Piazza IV Novembre, a beautiful square with an especially appealing fountain, the Fontana Maggiore, built in the late 13th century.

It is only a short drive farther south from Perugia to ASSISI. Even if it were not for the lingering warmth of the gentle St Francis, this would be a delightful spot: in fact, I think it is one of the most spectacular of all the hilltowns in Umbria. Perhaps there are a few too many souvenir shops, but this is a small price to pay for such a very special place. The town walls begin on the lower slopes of the valley and perfectly enclose the area as it climbs the steep hillside with a climax in an enormous crowning castle. Assisi is a marvelous town for walking: you will need sturdy shoes to wind your way up and down the puzzle of tiny streets. It is great fun. You will come across intriguing little lanes which open into small squares. When you stop to rest, there will be marvelous vistas of the breathtaking Umbrian fields stretching out below. There is the fabulous St Francis' Basilica which includes a monastery with a beautiful arcaded courtyard.

To savor the beauty of Assisi, it is fun to spend the night and, luckily, there are several excellent hotel choices. Beautifully situated with one of its walls forming a section of the piazza of the St Francis' Basilica is the HOTEL SUBASIO. This is not a deluxe hotel but it has much to entice the tourist. Perhaps its most splendid attribute is the view: from the vine covered dining terraces, there are splendid vistas of the glorious undulating Umbrian fields which seem to glow with a special radiance. Some of the bedrooms, too, have gorgeous views from their balconies. Definitely splurge and request one of the best rooms so you can capture each possible moment of this very beautiful scene.

*Hotel Subasio*
*Assisi*

While staying at Assisi, drive one day the short distance to TORGIANO where there is a splendid wine museum.  One would never dream that such a tiny town could boast such a stunning museum, but it is not a coincidence.  The Lungarotti family owns the vineyards for miles in every direction and, indeed, they must be a very clever and dedicated family.  They also own a delightful hotel in the center of town, LE TRE VASELLE.  In addition to overseeing the decoration of this exquisite hotel, Signore Lungarotti also collected artifacts pertaining to every aspect of the production of wine from the earliest days which are in the museum. The collection is spectacular, worthy of a detour by anyone interested in wines. Not only is the museum delightful, but the collection is so beautifully displayed that it is a joy to visit.

Although only a short drive from Assisi to Orvieto by the direct route, a sightseeing excursion is worthwhile.  If you drive south from Assisi you will soon come to SPOLETO, a very interesting town.  Not only is this another of the beautifully preserved medieval cities with a dramatic hilltop location, but it also has an almost unbelievable bridge.  Dating from the Roman days, it spans the deep ravine between Spoleto and the adjoining mountain. It is almost inconceivable that such a bridge could have been built over a Roman aqueduct existing in the 14th century. The bridge is 755 feet long and 262 feet high!  It is supported by a series of ten Gothic arches and has a fort at the far end as well as a balcony in the center.

Before leaving the vicinity of Spoleto, if you are a St Francis enthusiast, you certainly must make the short detour to visit MONTELUCO, where St Francis came to live as a hermit.  You will appreciate why he chose Monteluco after you twist to the top of the mountain and enjoy the glorious view of the surrounding hillsides covered with olive trees.

If you have not had your fill of walled villages, you might enjoy a brief stop, as you head west, at TODI, another of the tiny hilltop walled villages about midway between Spoleto and Orvieto.  However, do not linger too long in Todi because Orvieto is a real prize.

ORVIETO is spread across the top of a hill which drops down on every side in steep volcanic cliffs.  One wonders how the town could ever have been built.  At Orvieto's center is a glorious duomo dominating a beautiful piazza.  You may think you have seen enough stunning cathedrals, but this one is really special - brilliantly colored in intricate mosaic designs and accentuated by slender spirals stretching gracefully into the sky.

Also of great interest in Orvieto is the visit to another engineering feat, St Patrick's Well. This well, over 200 feet deep, was hewn out of solid volcanic rock to collect and store water in case of a siege.

Since your distance is so short between Orvieto and Sinalunga, instead of taking one of the major highways, explore the small back roads, winding through the countryside as you head north. As a goal, mark on the map the small town of PIENZA as your first target. It does not matter if you get a little lost. The scenery is beautiful and you will probably discover your own little walled village. One of my favorites is the marvelous small town of Pienza. It is just lovely. It has a pristine beauty and has no modern developments to interrupt the charm of this tiny town, surrounded by walls which cap the hilltop. Within the town you will find quaint little squares and a church built almost on the edge of the ramparts with a lovely terrace view. A few miles north of Pienza is the abbey of Monte Oliveto Maggiore, serenely situated among the cypress forest. Of special interest are the terra cottas adorning the entrance, created by the famous artist, Luca della Robbia. The cloisters contain frescoes portraying the life of St Benedict.

*Locanda dell'Amorosa*
*Sinalunga*

From the Abbey, drive east to the town of SINALUNGA where there is a very delightful hotel, the LOCANDA DELL'AMOROSA. This hotel, in addition to being a wonderful place to spend the night, is really a sightseeing experience. The road to the Locanda dell'Amorosa is lined on both sides with tall cypress trees through which you glimpse an expanse of vineyards. The town walls are actually the hotel's entrance, as the hotel is the town. Pass through the gate into a large courtyard and at its end is an exquisite little church. The wing of buildings to the left contains the bedrooms. The wing to the right houses the reception lounge and the dining room. In this same little "hotel-town" a delicious wine is bottled which you can sample at dinner. I know you will enjoy your stay here.

## DESTINATION III  PANZANO IN CHIANTI  VILLA LE BARONE

On your way to Panzano be sure to stop in SIENA, another of the strategically built walled hilltowns. This is a delightful city and deserves many hours to savor all its attributes. The ramparts are perfectly preserved with massive gates guarding a meticulously maintained medieval stronghold. Drive as close as you can to the main square and park your car. All the sightseeing can and should be done by foot. The giant piazza is a sight in itself: it is immense and, instead of being square, is fan shaped. All the streets surrounding the square end like the spokes of a giant wheel in the Piazza del Campo. The town hall monopolizes one side of the piazza with graceful arches embellished with the coat of arms of Siena. It is in this gigantic piazza that the colorful "Palio delle Contrade" takes place in July and August every year. The horse race is only a part of this colorful spectacle of medieval costumes, wonderful banners and parades. You can check for the exact dates, but the festivities extend beyond the actual date of the races. Also, Siena has one of Italy's most dramatic cathedrals, located a short walk from the Piazza del Campo. Not only is the cathedral striking - with its bold patterns of black and white marble - but it also houses a museum.

From Siena, continue north on the expressway and take the turnoff for SAN GIMIGNANO. Although you might think you are weary of walled towns, San Gimignano is quite unique and definitely worth a stop. What is so dramatic about San Gimignano is that at one time this small walled village was surrounded by 72 towers. During the Middle Ages it was a status symbol for noble families to each build personal towers for protection: the higher the tower, the greater the image of wealth and importance. It is amazing that fourteen of the original towers of San Gimignano are still standing. They make a striking silhouette soaring like skyscrapers against the sky. On a clear day, you can see them on the horizon from miles away. In addition to the romance of the towers, San Gimignano is a charming medieval village and there is an excellent restaurant (also a delightful hotel), LA CISTERNA, found on the main square.

*Villa le Barone*
*Panzano in Chianti*

From San Gimignano, head almost directly east to **PANZANO IN CHIANTI** where the prize of your journey, **VILLA LE BARONE**, awaits you. This is an exquisite small hotel encompassing all the joys that are Tuscany. This lovely villa was once the home of the Della Robbia family, and today is owned by the Duchess Visconti. The location is idyllic: the villa is set in lovely gardens and surrounded by vineyards. There is a welcoming pool. A terrace for dining overlooks a panorama of the Tuscany hills stretching for miles in the distance while another dining room is fashioned from the former stables. Breakfast and dinner are included in the price and reservations during the high season are usually accepted only for a stay of several days: but this is no problem...you will want to stay forever.

When it is time to complete your loop and return to Florence you will find it only about an hour's drive away in time but years away in mood from the tranquility of the Villa le Barone.

*Romantic Hilltowns of Tuscany & Umbria*

# Rome to Milan
## via the Italian Riviera

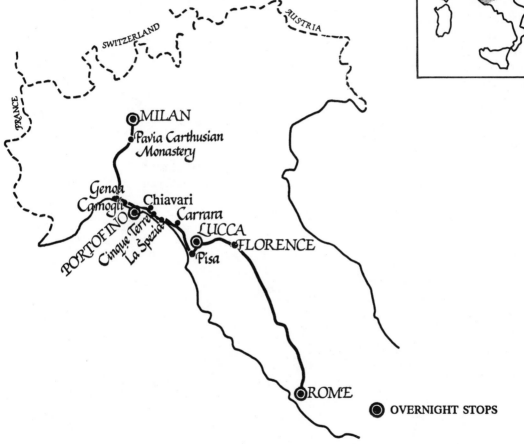

SWITZERLAND

AUSTRIA

FRANCE

⊙MILAN
•Pavia Carthusian
  Monastery

Genoa
Camogli
Chiavari
PORTOFINO
Cinque Terre
La Spezia
Carrara
LUCCA
Pisa
FLORENCE

⊙ROME

⊙ OVERNIGHT STOPS

# Rome to Milan via the Italian Riviera

This itinerary includes one of the most picturesque jewels of Italy - the Italian Riviera where not only are there charming towns snuggled into small coves along the shoreline, but also the road itself is a masterpiece of engineering. The coastal highway along the Riviera "bridges" for miles - high in the sky above the ravines - and "tunnels" in and out of the cliffs rising steeply from the sea.   The original title for this itinerary was "Coastal Route from Rome to Milan", but after we personally experienced the drive, the route and the name were changed.   There is an expressway partially following the coast from Rome to Pisa, but until this is finished the road is one of total frustration with a solid line of trucks and cars making the journey undesirable.   Far easier, and actually more scenic, is to take the expressway north from Rome to Florence through the gorgeous Tuscany hills then to head west on to Pisa and finally travel on via the coast to Genoa and Milan.   It is impossible to include all of the towns that dot the coastline, but after ducking on and off the freeway ourselves, we have tried to include some of the most charming.

## ORIGINATING CITY     ROME

This itinerary begins in ROME, a favorite of all and a wonderful introduction to Italy.   In the hotel section there are many suggestions for accommodations to suit your taste and budget.   When you are saturated with the overwhelming sights that Rome has to offer and are ready to continue your journey, buy an excellent map to assist you in maneuvering out of the city and onto the magnificent expressway heading north.

## DESTINATION I     LUCCA     HOTEL VILLA LA PRINCIPESSA

This itinerary assumes that you have already visited Florence, certainly one of the highlights of any Italian holiday.   If not, you will assuredly want to stop in Florence for several days.   Otherwise, when the expressway from Rome reaches Florence, take the major branch to the west and continue on toward PISA.   You will probably want to stop in Pisa for a few pictures of her Leaning Tower, but frankly I consider Pisa overrated.   It is such a solid mass of tourists and souvenir shops during the summer season that you can hardly find a place to park before trying to squirm your way to the central piazza.   I must admit that the duomo, gleaming white with its companion leaning tower, is impressive, so if you have never seen it, do stop.   But even more interesting and not nearly so "touristy" is the beautiful city of LUCCA located only a few miles to the north.   This too is an ancient city, even more perfectly preserved than its neighbor, Pisa.   Lucca has surrounding the city an enormous wall so wide that it even harbors delightful small parks and a road which runs along the top.   A drive along the top of these ramparts is a wonderful way to get a bird's eye view of this extremely picturesque medieval town before you park your car and explore on foot.

If you are driving from Pisa to Lucca there is a beautiful villa just to the west of the old road, only a few miles before you come to Lucca. The VILLA LA PRINCIPESSA is a gorgeous palace-style hotel set in a beautiful park with a delightful swimming pool which is a welcome bonus after a long day of sightseeing. The inside of the villa is, in my estimation, somewhat wild in its choice of colors for decor, but the setting is so magnificent and the building so beautiful that I highly recommend it.

*Villa la Principessa*
*Lucca*

DESTINATION II          PORTOFINO          HOTEL SPLENDIDO

When you leave the Villa la Principessa, head back to the expressway and continue north.  What looks like glaciers soon shimmers white in the foothills of the Apuan Alps which rise to the right of the highway.  This is not snow at all, but rather your introduction to the beautiful white Italian marble.  You might enjoy a detour to visit some of the marble mines.  Exit the highway at CARRARA and take the winding drive up into the hills to the ancient village of COLONNATA - famous through the ages for its marvelous white marble.  As you wander this tiny town you will be following the footsteps of the perfectionist, Michelangelo, who used to come to Carrara personally to choose huge blocks of marble from which to carve his masterpieces.

Leaving Carrara you will enjoy an adventure of an entirely different kind - exploring the five little isolated towns on the coast called CINQUE TERRE. This area is quickly becoming linked with civilization so if you love the thrill of discovering old fishing villages still untouched by time do not tarry.

To begin this portion of your journey take the small road from Carrara west returning to the main highway and continuing on to the port of LA SPEZIA, a large sea port and navy town.  From here you might want to take the short drive to the tip of the peninsula south of Spezia to visit the old fishing village of PORTOVERERE which clings to the steep rocks rising from the sea. This was one of Lord Byron's haunts when he lived across the bay at San Terenzo.  You will then need to return to La Spezia to continue your journey.

The Cinque Terre used to be five completely isolated fishing villages on a stretch of land between La Spezia to the south and Levanto to the north.  First only a footpath connected these hamlets, then a train was installed, and now real civilization is encroaching with a road under construction which will open them all to the world of tourism.  Three of the towns are accessible now by road.  From La Spezia you can travel to RIOMAGGIORE and then on to MANOROLA.  From the northern approach of Levanto you can travel by road to the first town of MONTEROSSO.  Still completely cut off from car traffic are the ancient fishing hamlets between - VERNAZZA and CORNIGLIA. It is best to drive as far as possible from La Spezia stopping first at Riomaggiore and then on to Manorola. Upon arrival you can let your mood, the time, and the weather dictate your explorations.  You can continue on by hiking the spectacular trails connecting the villages, by taking the small ferry between them, by using the train - or, best yet, combine them all.   If you have time to see only one of the scenic towns, Vernazza, which clings perilously to a rocky promontory forming a tiny harbor, is perhaps the most scenic.

After Cinque Terre continue north along the coast.   If you are in a hurry return to the freeway A 12.   If time is not a problem, continue along the coast via the towns of SESTRI LEVANTE and CHIAVARI to SAN MARGHERITA.   Here you take the small road south for the short drive to the "picture book" village of PORTOFINO.   This last section of the road, especially in summer, is jammed with traffic, but the plum at the end is worth the hassle.   Portofino certainly has already been discovered but it is so delightful it deserves its accolades.

*Hotel Splendido*
*Portofino*

As you approach Portofino watch for the entrance sign for the HOTEL SPLENDIDO.   There is a guard at the entrance and only those with reservations are allowed to follow the little road as it winds up the hill to the magnificent villa style hotel. The Splendido is a deluxe hotel: a very expensive hotel whose prices include breakfast and dinner. But what a gorgeous setting! The hotel is perched in the hills above the town with splendid views of the sea and the harbor. A beautiful swimming pool nestles below the hotel and tennis courts are found in the gardens to the left. There are enchanting little trails threading their way throughout the gardens which surround the hotel. Along the paths benches are strategically positioned for quiet moments to savor the stunning view. It is an easy walk into Portofino if you can bear to leave your oasis.

Portofino is considered a national treasure and it truly is a jewel. Her tiny harbor is filled with gorgeous yachts, small ferries, and colorful fishing boats. In the center of town is a delightful small square. Enveloping the harbor are colorful tall and narrow fishermen's cottages painted in warm colors of siennas, ochres, and pinks with green shutters. Bright flower boxes accent the windows and the laundry flaps gaily in the breeze. Vivid reflections of these quaint little houses shimmer in the emerald water. Beyond the town the heavily forested, beautiful green hills rise steeply to complete this idyllic scene.

*NOTE:* While staying in Portofino, we highly recommend a short drive south to one of Italy's finest restaurants, the CA'PEO, located in Chiavari a Leivi. You must make prior reservations because Franco and his wife Melly only take guests who call ahead since all of the food is specially prepared depending upon how many will be dining: telephone (0185) 319 090. The Ca'Peo, whose origins date back to a very old farmhouse, is located high in the hills overlooking the coast. Also, if you love fine food and prefer to visit Portofino instead of overnighting there, you might want to spend several nights at the much more reasonably priced Ca'Peo which has a few suites. (See page 118.)

DETOUR NOTE:   For those of you traveling to the French Riviera, we wish you "adieu" in Portofino.   From there you will continue to follow the coastal highway west to Genoa along the Italian Riviera into France, to the French Riviera and across to the principality of Monaco.

For the rest of "our group", after leaving Portofino return to the main highway and continue west for about 18 miles to Genoa.   Bypass Genoa and instead, as you circle the city, watch for the freeway to the north going to Milan.

An enjoyable detour on your way north is the PAVIA CARTHUSIAN MONASTERY (Certosa di Pavia).   Probably the simplest way to find it would be to watch for the turnoff to Pavia (about 60 miles north of Genoa).   At this point take the road east to Pavia and from there go north about 5 miles to the Carthusian Monastery.   Lavishly built in the 15th century, this splendid monastery is claimed by some to be one of the finest buildings in Italy. (Check carefully the days and hours open - it is usually closed on Mondays and for several hours midday).   The outside of the monastery is lavishly designed with colorful marble and intricate designs.   Inside, the small cloisters are especially charming with 122 arches framed by beautiful terra cotta moldings.   There is also a baroque fountain within, plus several small gardens.   Next to the monastery the Palace of the Dukes of Milan has been turned into a museum.

After your tour of the monastery it is approximately 16 miles farther north to MILAN.   Milan has many large, sophisticated city-style hotels, but if you enjoy a smaller, less commercial place to stay, we recommend the ANTICA LOCANDA SOLFERINO.   This small hotel is famous as one of Milan's most charming small restaurants.   But, luckily for the traveller, there are tucked upstairs a few simple, pleasantly decorated guest rooms which are very attractively priced.

*Antica Locanda Solferino*
*Milan*

You can walk from the Antica Locanda Solferino to most of the places of interest. If you enjoy shopping (and Milan has some of the finest in Italy) you must not miss the splendid glass-domed shopping arcade, lined with beautiful boutiques and cozy cafes. After a stroll through the arcade, you emerge into an imposing square dominated by the truly spectacular DUOMO, the third largest cathedral in the world. Not only is the size impressive, but this is also a sensational cathedral with a marble facade enhanced by over 100 slender spires piercing the sky. And every opera buff knows about Milan's fabulous theater, LA SCALA. Even if you have not been an opera enthusiast in the past, if you are in Milan during the opera season (which usually runs from December to May) write ahead and try to get tickets - the theater is stunning and an experience not to be missed. So, although Milan is a sprawling, overwhelming metropolis, if you can find your way to her medieval core, you will find an intriguing city, well worth a visit.

*Rome to Milan via the Italian Riviera*

# Highlights of
# Southern Italy & Sicily

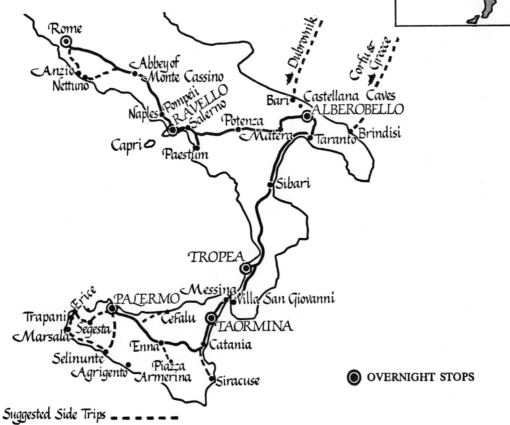

Rome

Anzio
Nettuno

Abbey of
Monte Cassino

Naples
Pompeii
RAVELLO
Salerno

Capri

Paestum

Potenza

Matera

Dubrovnik

Bari

Castellana Caves
ALBEROBELLO

Corfu & Greece

Taranto

Brindisi

Sibari

TROPEA

PALERMO

Messina

Villa San Giovanni

Erice

Trapani

Cefalu

TAORMINA

Marsala

Segesta

Enna

Catania

Selinunte

Agrigento

Piazza
Armerina

Siracuse

Suggested Side Trips ━ ━ ━ ━

⦿ OVERNIGHT STOPS

77

# Highlights of Southern Italy & Sicily

Having visited the famous trio of Rome, Florence, and Venice, most tourists think that they have "seen" Italy. If childhood geography lessons call forth such names as Pompeii, Herculaneum and Paestum, all too frequently the urge to visit these jewels of archaeological wonders is lost in the misconception that southern Italy is an uninteresting destination. What a waste. Southern Italy has fascinating ruins, gorgeous coastlines, beautiful medieval walled villages, lovely beaches, marvelous hilltowns, and some of the most unusual sights in Italy. Best yet, what fun to return home and casually mention to your dinner partner, who thinks he has been everywhere, that you think the Emerald Grotto on the Amalfi coast far exceeds the beauty of the Blue Grotto of Capri or that the Greek ruins at Paestum outshine many found in Greece or that the mysterious town of Alberobello still haunts you.

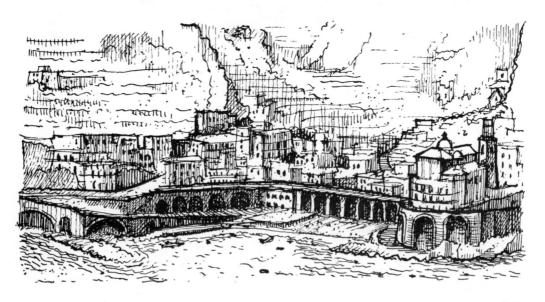

Therefore, for those of you who have already seen the fantastic highlights of northern Italy, we take pleasure in presenting to you the best of southern Italy. This itinerary makes a circle of southern Italy in order to suit the travel needs of a wide selection of tourists. Follow the entire route or select the portion best for you since this itinerary lends itself especially well for the traveller who wants to take only a segment. As an example, the journey from Rome to Brindisi is a popular one for the lucky tourist on his way to Greece. Or the west coast is a popular drive for the tourist who wants to visit Sicily and then return to Rome by air or ferry. And most popular of all is the segment from Rome to the Amalfi Drive. So, this itinerary allows you to custom tailor your journey and gives you many wonderful tips on what to see along the way.

## ORIGINATING CITY       ROME

ROME is a most convenient starting point to begin a tour of southern Italy. Rome Airport is the destination of planes from all over the world and here passengers begin their "Roman holiday". In Rome one can one's soul in the wealth of history, art, architecture, museums, and monuments - and build a foundation for the sights which will be encountered on the journey.

Because there is such a wide selection of accommodations in Rome in various price categories and locations, it seems most practical for you to choose the hotel that best suits your personality and budget from the hotel description section in the back of this guide. You will find that Rome has a wealth of excellent hotels and, even though the city is large, amazingly most of the hotels are within walking distance of both shopping and sightseeing highlights. Or, if you do not like to walk, ask the concierge at your desk to call you a taxi or direct you to the nearest subway station. (Rome's main subway line stretches across the city - conveniently connecting most of the places of interest for the tourist.)

Rome always has a monumental traffic problem. Within the city look for strategically located signs that indicate that there is a freeway ahead. It might be quite a distance, but be patient as these signs will lead you to the outskirts of Rome where there is a highway encircling the city. Follow the freeway around to the exit for the major expressway heading south, Highway A2. When you reach this expressway continue south for approximately 80 miles to the exit for CASSINO. Actually you will be able to spot your destination from several miles away because the ABBEY OF MONTE CASSINO crowns the top of a large mountain to the left of the highway as you drive south. When you reach Cassino turn off the expressway and about midway through town the road that winds up the summit of the mountain to the Abbey of Monte Cassino is clearly marked. This abbey, founded by St Benedict in 529AD, is extremely interesting both religiously and historically. For war historians the abbey is very significant because this is where the Germans held out against the Allied forces for almost a year in World War II. When the mountain was finally conquered in May 1944 it opened the way for Allied forces to move into Rome. As you read your history books it seems strange that one fort could hold out for so long, but when you see the abbey you understand. It is an enormous building on the crest of a precipitous mountain. In the siege the abbey was almost destroyed but it has been rebuilt according to the original plans and is very impressive.

NOTE: For those of you who for sentimental or historical reasons are especially interested in World War II there is another destination you might well want to visit in this day's journey. ANZIO is a town on the coast about 35 miles south of Rome and could easily be included as a stop before Cassino. It was at Anzio that the British and the Americans landed in January 1944. The emotional reminder of this terrible war is a few miles south at NETTUNO where 8,000 white crosses and stars of David flow - row after row across the green lawn. There is a circular drive around the parklike grounds which are beautifully maintained. A memorial chapel and small war museum are located at the end of the grounds. For those who lost family or friends during the invasion there is an office to the right as you drive in where you can find out where your loved ones are buried.

From Cassino return to the expressway and continue south for about 37 miles until you see the sign for POMPEII. Unless you have absolutely NO interest in archaeology you must stop in Pompeii, the city of your childhood geography books, where time was frozen for 25,000 people under the ashes from the eruption of Vesuvius in the year 62. Some of the sites within Pompeii are still under repair from the destruction wrought by the mighty 1980 earthquake, but do not let this deter you. There is so much to see that you will never feel cheated by nature's mischief. (If you are REALLY into archaeology you must also visit the NATIONAL ARCHAEOLOGICAL MUSEUM in Naples where many of the artifacts from Pompeii are housed in a magnificent museum.)

Time slips back 2,000 years as you wander the streets of Pompeii and visit the temples, the lovely homes, the wine shops, bakery, public baths, etc. There is probably no other place where you can feel so strongly the pulse of ancient days. Many of the private homes have been reconstructed so you can marvel at the lovely inner courtyards, beautiful dining rooms in Pompeii red with intricate paintings on the walls, fountains, servants' quarters, bath rooms, and gardens. At the entrance to Pompeii there are souvenir stands where you can purchase a guide book to the city, or, if you prefer, you can hire a private guide at the entrance. Pompeii is so fascinating that you might well want to come back to spend a complete day visiting the city and the nearby ruins of Herculaneum which are also extremely interesting.

Leaving Pompeii, head to the coast in the direction of Sorrento where the AMALFI DRIVE, which must be one of the most beautiful stretches of coast in the world, begins. Be sure to time your journey when there is sufficient daylight because not only do you not want to miss any of the vistas, but the road is extremely twisty and precipitous and you will be glad of the best visibility.

There are many excellent choices for hotels along the Amalfi Drive. Concentrated in just a few miles are some of the most splendid hotels, both budget and luxury, in all of Italy. It is hard to recommend just one since each is unique. One of my favorite towns is the cliff-clinging village of RAVELLO, reached by a road which twists and winds its way up and up and up and then suddenly delivers you in a little village high in the clouds with absolutely dazzling views.

*Hotel Palumbo*
*Ravello*

In Ravello there are several wonderful inns - all of which can be heartily recommended, but none can surpass the delightful PALUMBO. You enter into a lovely light and airy reception room brimming with flowers and sunlight. Tucked throughout the inn are cozy little nooks filled with antiques. The inside dining room is charming, but usually meals are taken outside to enjoy to the maximum the surrounding scenery: steep hills covered with vineyards flowing down to the rugged coast where brilliant blue water dances between the rocks. The garden terrace of the Palumbo is an oasis of beauty and quiet enhanced by spectacular views. On an upper level is still another rooftop terrace where the sun and views are trapped again for the lucky guest. The Palumbo is not a luxury hotel, but what a jewel.

*Highlights of Southern Italy & Sicily*

Before leaving Ravello you will certainly want to visit some of the other small fishing villages which dot the coast, such as POSITANO and AMALFI. These towns during the season are bursting with tourists, but fun to see.

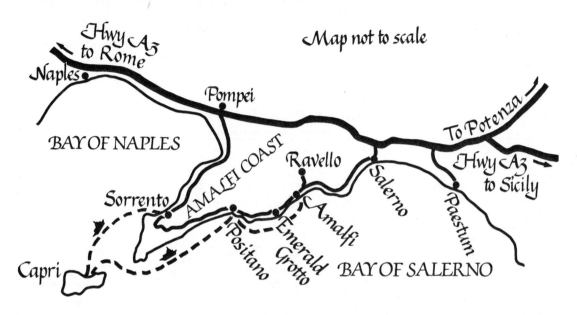

Also, if you have not been able to include an interlude on Capri during your Italian holiday I would suggest an excursion to this enchanted island located just off the coast. Steamers and hydrofoils depart regularly from Sorrento, Amalfi, and Positano. Ask at the tourist bureau or at your hotel for the schedule. (When the seas are rough it is more difficult to leave from Positano since there is no pier and it becomes necessary to take a small boat from the shore to the ferry.)

Also along the Amalfi coast is the EMERALD GROTTO, located between the towns of Amalfi and Positano. After parking, you buy a ticket and descend by elevator down the steep cliff to a small rocky terrace. Upon entering the cave which is filled with water, you will be rowed about the grotto in a small boat while your guide explains how the shimmering green water is formed by a secret tunnel allowing sunlight to filter from deep below the surface. The cave is filled with colorful stalactites and stalagmites which further enhance the mysterious mood. There is also a nativity scene below the water which magically appears and then drifts again from view.

| DESTINATION II | ALBEROBELLO | DEI TRULLI HOTEL |

When it is time to leave Ravello, there is an efficient expressway south to the "toe" of Italy. But for those who are en route to Brindisi or who have the luxury of time for another adventure, I am going to include a detour to the eastern coast, to the wondrous town of ALBEROBELLO.

I suggest an early start as there are several sightseeing stops recommended enroute. First of all, I definitely would make the short side trip south to visit the spectacular ancient Greek city of PAESTUM. To reach Paestum take the Amalfi coastal road from Ravello to Salerno and then join the expressway for about 12 miles until the turnoff for Paestum which is located on a side road about a half-hour drive from the freeway. Magically, as soon as you go through the gates of the ancient city you enter a peaceful environment of a lovely country meadow whose grass is dotted with some of the world's best preserved Greek temples. As you walk the remains of the streets criss-crossing the city, your senses are enhanced by birds singing and the scent of roses. It is a delightful experience. (Before leaving Paestum you might want to stop for a snack at a lovely restaurant, MARINI SEA GARDEN, which is in a garden whose gates open onto the west side of the excavation. The Marini Sea Garden restaurant is an old villa with an attractive dining room plus a garden terrace cafe.)

When you rejoin the expressway continue east for about 14 miles until the highway splits.   At this point take the left branch heading east toward Potenza.   About 70 miles beyond the branch of the highway, watch for the exit leading to the town of MATERA.   Located about a half-hour drive north of the expressway, Matera is a strange, spooky, ghost town with a weird setting amongst ravines and deep gorges. The old town of Matera clings to the side of a hill crowned by a modern city.   To visit the lower "lost city" whose crumbling buildings melt into the rocks is a fascinating experience.

From Matera continue on the road leading northeast to Alberobello.   Here are some of the strangest structures in Italy - the TRULLI.   These are circular stone buildings, usually built in small clusters, standing crisply white with conical slate roofs and whimsical twisted chimneys.   Outside ladders frequently lead to upper stories.   Often several of these houses are joined together to form a larger complex.   The houses are intertwined with cobbled streets.   What a strange and fascinating sight!   These conical little houses form a jumble of a small village which looks as though it should be inhabited by elves instead of "real" people.

*Trulli Houses*

For a hotel choice, you should certainly choose the DEI TRULLI. This hotel is located right on the outskirts of the trulli village and is built within the ancient houses. The hotel is a cluster of some of the round little houses which are made into cottages scattered within a large parklike setting. Pine trees line the small paths which join the hotel rooms. Each bungalow has a living room with fireplace, one or more bedrooms, a bathroom, and small patio. One of the trulli houses has been made into a dining room and another into the office. There is also a swimming pool and a tiny park with play equipment for the children.

*Hotel dei Trulli*
*Alberobello*

The trulli houses are not confined to the town of Alberobello although this is where you will find them composing an entire village. In fact, the trulli houses you will see in the vicinity of Alberobello are sometimes more interesting than those in the town itself. As you drive along the small roads you will spot gorgeous villas cleverly converted from trulli houses that are now obviously the homes of wealthy Italians. Others are now farmhouses with goats munching their lunch in the front yard. Occasionally you will spot a charming old trulli home cozily nestled in the center of a vineyard.   But most fun of all are the trulli homes of the free spirits. Their homes, instead of displaying the typical white exteriors, have been painted a brilliant yellow or pink or bright green with contrasting shutters.

As you are exploring the countryside around Alberobello you might want to take the short drive north to see the CASTELLANA CAVES where in a two-hour tour you will see many rooms of richly colored stalagmites and stalactites.


## DESTINATION III            TROPEA            BAIA PARAELIOS

NOTE: Alberobello is only about 45 miles from BRINDISI, the popular port from which to take the ferry to Corfu and on to Greece, and only about 35 miles from BARI which is the port to use for ferries to Dubrovnik.   So, if your plans are to continue your travel adventures by boat, then Alberobello is most strategically positioned.   In both Bari and Brindisi you can turn in your rental car if your holiday in Italy has ended.

However, for the rest of "our tour" the itinerary continues on to the exciting destination of Sicily.   When you leave Alberobello take the road south to the coast. You might want to make a stop to see the ancient port of TARANTO which is connected by a bridge to the modern city of Taranto.   Even if you are not interested in ancient history you might enjoy seeing the Italian naval ships - giant grey monsters sitting in the protected harbor.

From Taranto continue along the arch of Italy's boot until you come to Sibari where there is a short road leading east to join the main expressway.   When you are again on the Highway A3 continue south for only a few miles until you come to the exit for the tiny spur which juts up from the toe of Italy's boot and continue along the coast toward the town of TROPEA, located near the point of the peninsula.

*Baia Paraelios*
*Tropea - Parghelia*

Just before Tropea, a sign on the right of the road points to the HOTEL BAIA PARAELIOS, a very special hotel creating a wonderful combination of a beach holiday with your sightseeing.   The hotel is a cluster of cottages, cleverly spaced at various levels leading down to the beach.   Each cottage has a sitting room and one or more bedrooms plus a private terrace.   Although the hotel is not old, a definite "inn" feeling prevails.   The small reception room at the crest of the slope has lovely prints on the wall, baskets of flowers, a few antiques, and the definite flavor of good taste.   The cottages are quite appealing with tiled floors and earth tone colors. There is a swimming pool on one of the "mid" levels plus at beach edge nice chairs and a delightful dining room with an outdoor terrace for summer meals.   However, I saved the best for last - stretching in front of the hotel is a beautiful creamy-white sand beach.   Just a few miles beyond the hotel (which is officially located in the town of Parghelia - which is so small it never shows up on any maps) is the town of Tropea.   An ancient fishing village, Tropea is perched on cliffs overhanging the beautiful blue sea.   The town is most colorful and definitely worth a visit.

# Sicily

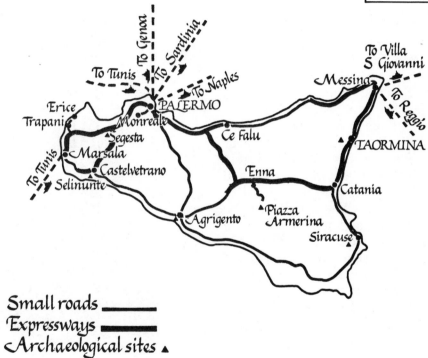

To Genoa
To Sardinia
To Tunis
To Naples
To Villa
S Giovanni
Messina
To Reggio
Erice
Trapani
PALERMO
Monreale
Ce Falu
TAORMINA
Segesta
Marsala
To Tunis
Castelvetrano
Selinunte
Enna
Catania
Agrigento
Piazza
Armerina
Siracuse

Small roads ____
Expressways ▬▬▬
Archaeological sites ▲

# Sicily

You can end your holiday savoring the beauty of Italy's southern coast, enjoying the tranquil beauty of the deserted beaches and the inviting clear water. However, Sicily beckons, just a short drive and boatride away. Sicily is truly a treasure of ancient monuments - a must for those who love archaeology. The continuation of this itinerary crosses the narrow channel leading from the tip of the toe over to this island of Sicily.

Upon leaving Baia Paraelios, return to the expressway and continue south the short distance to the tip of the toe and take the exit to Villa San Giovanni. The route to the ferry is clearly marked. The boat ferries leave at least twice an hour for **MESSINA**, Sicily. After buying your ticket you drive your car to the indicated lane and wait with all the trucks and campers and other cars for the signal to drive onto the boat. When on board you can leave your car and go upstairs to a lounge area where snacks can be purchased while traversing the short channel. In half an hour, the large ferry draws up to the pier in Messina and you drive off to experience some of the most beautifully preserved Greek ruins to be found anywhere in the world.

When the ferry arrives in MESSINA follow the freeway signs to TAORMINA, about a half-hour drive south. Once in town watch for signs to the SAN DOMENICO PALACE which commands a dramatic perch overlooking the sea. The San Domenico Palace is a museum-quality monastery which has been exquisitely converted into a deluxe hotel. Stunning antiques, appropriate to the period, are seen in every nook and corner. If you listen carefully, you can almost hear the soft chant of hooded monks quietly meditating as they walk through the arcaded courtyard. However, the superb amenities of today have been discreetly interspersed and even a swimming pool now nestles in the garden.

*San Domenico Palace*
*Taormina*

The town of Taormina is also delightful. As if glued to the top of a small peninsula, Taormina juts out to the sea and then drops steeply to the coast below. Quaint, colorful streets wind through the town where you can browse in the gift shops, visit small churches, enjoy a cappuccino at a little cafe, or simply enjoy the view.

## DESTINATION V     PALERMO     GRAND HOTEL VILLA IGIEA

From Taormina follow the freeway south toward CATANIA. Be forewarned that the freeway bypassing the city is not yet finished and until it is you will have to follow a maze of streets as signs lead you through the congested traffic. Have hope though. Finally you will emerge at the outskirts of the city where the freeway continues on to Palermo. Before heading for Palermo you might want to take the approximately 80-mile roundtrip excursion south to SYRACUSE which is an ancient Greek city dating back to 700BC. The Greeks loved beauty and here overlooking a gorgeous blue bay they built their theaters, temples, and coliseums. Of special interest is an enormous theater over 400 feet across.

Enna is about an hour's drive west from Catania. Should you want to include another short detour, about 20 miles south of Enna is the town of PIAZZA ARMERINA, about 4 miles southwest of which there are some excellent mosaics in the remains of an ancient Roman villa - the VILLA OF CASALE. Returning to Enna take the expressway north toward the coast and then head west to PALERMO.

Palermo is a large city with lots of traffic and new construction. However, it makes a good base from which to explore some of the jewels of Sicily and luckily there is a splendid hotel here, the GRAND HOTEL VILLA IGIEA. Actually, the hotel is much more like a small castle than a villa and is an oasis in a bustling city.

The hotel is located on the ocean right next to the harbor. The entrance is rather formal and grand. The bedrooms are large and nicely furnished in a traditional motif and those in the rear have a lovely view over the back garden to the sea. There is a pool in the garden which even sports its own miniature Greek temple.

*Grand Hotel Villa Igiea*
*Palermo*

From Palermo there are many fascinating excursions. A circle trip from Palermo includes some of Sicily's finest archaeological sites. To begin your journey take the expressway west toward TRAPANI. About 5 miles after the highway splits you will see a sign for SEGESTA which is located only a few minutes from the expressway. Here in a remote mountain area stands a delightful Greek Doric temple - practically perfect in its preservation. In fact, many experts consider this to be one of the finest Greek Doric temples in the world today. But one of the most superb aspects of this temple is its location: there is nothing to jar the senses. Reached by a path leading up from the parking area, the temple is located on a small hill with great natural beauty all around. After visiting the temple return to the parking area and follow the signs up the hill for another treat - a small, but beautiful Greek theater. Again, the location is what makes this theater so special. What an eye the Greeks had for beauty. The stage is set in such a way that the spectators look out across the mountains to the sea.

Just north of Trapani is the ancient town of ERICE perched on rocks soaring over 2,000 feet in the clouds. This is a fascinating walled city filled with colorful medieval houses.

South of Trapani the road circles the island and passes through MARSALA which gives its name to the famous Marsala wine of the region.

The next destination is the great Greek ruins at SELINUNTE. As you near Castelvetrano watch for signs for the coastal archaeological site. Here by the ocean are the impressive remains of some of the most gigantic temples left by the Greeks. It is staggering to imagine how the Greeks more than 2,500 years ago could have pieced together the huge blocks of rock weighing over 100 tons each. From Selinunte the expressway heads directly north for your return to Palermo.

Another recommended side trip from Palermo would be to visit the ancient fishing village of CEFALU built on a rocky peninsula about an hour's drive east from Palermo. Not only is this a very colorful fishing village complete with brightly hued boats and twisting narrow streets, but there is also a splendid Norman cathedral built by King Roger in the 12th century in fulfillment of a promise to God for sparing his life during a storm at sea.

Two of Palermo's major sights are luckily only a few miles from the city. In MONREALE, about 5 miles south, is an awesome cathedral which is especially famous for its beautiful mosaic panels showing a strong Moorish influence. Reading from left to right these 130 pictures depict the complete cycle of both the Old and the New Testaments. The bronze doors of the cathedral are also beautiful and were designed by Bonanno Pisano, a famous 12th-century artist.

The other sight close to Palermo is MONTE PELLEGRINO, just west of the city. Here is a cave which has been transformed into a chapel commemorating Santa Rosalia, a Duke's daughter who became a hermit - living and dying in this cave.

There is still another very important archaeological site on Sicily - the ruins of the VALLEY OF THE TEMPLES at ARRGIGENTO.   There is no doubt that this ancient Greek city, with the Temple of Juno, the Temple of Concord, the Temple of Hercules, the Temple of Jupiter and the Temple of the Dioscuri, is a marvelous example of the tremendous wealth, power and skills of the ancient Greeks. Because this excursion takes such a long drive of which only a short portion is freeway and because there is no excellent inn to recommend for the night, it seems that the wealth of temples that are more easily accessible will probably suffice for all but the most ardent ancient Greek enthusiast. When it is time to leave Sicily Palermo is a convenient gateway.   From here you can fly back to Rome making a connection to your homeward flight or else you can take a ferry back to Naples, Genoa, Sardinia, or even Tunis.

96          *Hotel Map Index*

*Italy*

- Bolzano
- 10
- 11
- 8
- 9
- 5
- 6
- 23 22
- 21
- 7
- 25
- 24
- 20
- 19
- 13 12
- 4
- 3
- 1
- 26
- Milan
- 14
- 16
- 2
- 15
- 17
- 18
- Venice
- 27
- Genoa
- 37
- 28
- 30
- 29
- 31
- 32
- 34
- 33
- 35
- 36
- 38
- Florence
- 39
- 40
- 42
- 43
- 46
- 44
- 49
- 47
- 45
- 41
- 50
- Assisi
- Siena
- 48
- 51
- 52
- 53
- 54
- 55
- 56
- Rome
- 57
- 67
- Naples
- 59
- 58
- 60
- 61
- Brindisi
- 62
- 63
- 64
- 66
- 65

97

There is a fascinating section in southeastern Italy with a collection of strange round white buildings with grey stone conical shaped roofs.   These ancient houses seem to be "left over" from some Moorish tribe which must have inhabited this part of Italy long ago.   These houses are called "trulli" and are usually seen in groups of two or three.   In the town of Alberobello there is actually a whole village of the conical little houses whose jumble of domed roofs, whitewashed walls, and crooked little chimneys create a most unusual sight.   Fortunately there is a superb hotel in the area that is located within walking distance of the trulli village.   Not only is its location excellent, but the hotel captures the mood of the area since it is constructed within some of the ancient trulli houses.  Small bungalows are scattered around a large parklike area connected by winding pathways under the pine trees.   Each bungalow is actually a suite with a modern bathroom, a living room with fireplace, one or more bedrooms, and a private patio.   The suites are spacious but the decor quite simple.   The dining rooms and the reception area each occupy their own "trulli".   Within the grounds a pool and children's play yard have been added.   If you are on your way to Greece or Yugoslavia you will find the Hotel dei Trulli an excellent choice since it is very close to Brindisi and Bari, the two major ferry ports.

*HOTEL DEI TRULLI*
*Manager: Luigi Farace*
*Via Cadore*
*70011 Alberobello, Italy*
*tel: (080) 721 130 or 721 044*
*34 rooms: Lire 220,000 (includes 2 meals)*
*Closed during winter months*
*Near the "heel" of Italy*
*Swimming pool - small park*
*Located 68 km NW of Brindisi*

The Villa Cipriani is just as I had envisioned in every dream of Italy: an old villa snuggled on a hill; her softly faded exterior emphasized by dark green shutters; masses of roses creeping over trellises; columns adorned with vines; lazy views over rolling green hills; faded ochre-colored walls half hidden by tall cypress trees dotting nearby hilltops; birds singing in the garden; the sentimental rhythmical peal of church bells; a pianist on the terrace playing old love songs; the fragrance of flowers drifting through the air like the finest perfume; a balmy night under the stars - perfection.  My impression of a romantic paradise must not have been a unique experience for in the garden was a wedding party.  A beautiful bride - a handsome groom; they had fallen in love at the Cipriani and had returned with family and friends from the United States for their marriage.  The Villa Cipriani is located in Asolo, a charming, small, medieval, walled hill town less than two hours northwest of Venice.  It has an atmosphere so delightful that Robert Browning chose it as a residence.  And the home he chose?  The Cipriani.  Luckily, the home is now a hotel and you, too, can "live" in Asolo.

*HOTEL VILLA CIPRIANI*
*Manager: Giuseppe Kamenar*
*Via Canova, 298*
*31011 Asolo, Italy*
*tel: (0423) 55 444 telex: 411060*
*32 rooms: Lire 246,000 - 317,000*
*Credit cards: All major*
*Open: All year*
*U.S. Rep: CIGA, 800-221- 2340*
*Beautiful old villa*
*Located 65 km NW of Venice*

One of the joys of researching a guidebook is to discover a "jewel" of an inn - it is rather like a treasure hunt.   Rarely though do we find an excellent hotel which we have not heard of previously.   However, the Country House, located on a small lane less than half a mile from the lower gates into Assisi, is just such a find.   The inn is actually an ancient peasant's cottage which Silvana Ciammarvghi, the owner, has lovingly restored and transformed into a small pension.   It is not surprising that the hotel is so loaded with charm, for Silvana loves antiques and has an eye for beautiful wooden chests, tables, chairs, mirrors and beds.   In fact, the first floor of this inn is an antique shop.   Most of the furniture in the house is for sale but, no problem: when a piece is sold, another takes its place from the shop downstairs. All of the rooms have style and taste and are decorated with an antique "country" ambiance.   When we first visited the Antichita "Three Esse" Country House it had only recently opened.   On our last visit many improvements had been made making this small inn even more attractive.   Silvana was there to greet us again and was as charming as ever.   She speaks excellent English and will be glad to welcome you to her "home" which would make an excellent location for exploring Umbria.

*ANTICHITA "THREE ESSE" COUNTRY HOUSE*
*Owner: Silvana Ciammarvghi*
*S. Pietro*
*06081 Assisi, Italy*
*tel: (075) 816 363*
*12 rooms: Lire 56,000*
*Breakfast only served*
*Open: All year*
*Inn combined with antique shop*
*Countryside location near Assisi*
*Located 177 km N of Rome*

The Hotel Subasio is located in Assisi with one wall forming part of the ancient square in front of the Basilica of St. Francis. In fact, the hotel is actually linked to the Basilica by an arched colonnade. The setting is marvelous, with the rear of the hotel facing the beautiful Umbrian countryside. On the lower level there are several delightful view terraces romantically shaded by vines. Many of the rooms also have splendid views over the Umbrian valley. Request one of the deluxe rooms with a view balcony - these are delightful. The public rooms of the Subasio are pleasant, but rather stilted and formal. However, you will not be inside much anyway. The terraces are magic: to sit and watch the lovely fields mellow in the evening sun with that very special glow which is so characteristic of Umbria is certainly one of life's real pleasures. It is no wonder that many celebrities have chosen the Hotel Subasio for residence when visiting Assisi; such famous names as Charlie Chaplin and James Stewart grace the guest book, and it certainly deserves its wonderful reputation. Andrea Rossi personally oversees the management of the hotel and there is a friendliness in the air from the gentle maid who turns down your bed in the evening to the charming waiter who helps select your local wine with dinner.

*HOTEL SUBASIO*
*Owner: Andrea E. Rossi*
*Via Frate Ella, 2*
*06081 Assisi, Italy*
*tel: (075) 812 206 telex: 662029*
*70 rooms: Lire 128,000*
*Open: All year*
*Credit cards: All major*
*Located about 177 km N of Rome*

For a splendid, moderately priced little inn just off the Piazza del Commune in the heart of Assisi, the Hotel Umbra is a wonderful choice. If you are expecting a luxury hotel with fancy decor, this will not be the hotel for you. Although the public rooms have accents of antiques and a cozy ambiance, they are "homey" rather than grand. The bedrooms, which are clean and fresh, are simple rather than deluxe. Nevertheless, because of the absolutely delightful small terrace at the entrance which is oozing with charm, the Umbra would have won my heart even if the inside had been a disaster. You reach the Umbra by way of a narrow little alley leading off from the Piazza del Commune. The entrance is through wrought iron gates which open to a tiny patio - a green oasis of peace and quiet where tables are set under a trellis covered with vines whose leaves provide shade and paint a lacy pattern of shadows. From this intimate terrace there is a lovely view. Some of the bedrooms, too, have a panoramic vista of the Umbrian hills and valley. There is a cute little dining room and several small drawing rooms. This small, family owned and managed hotel is a real asset to the wonderful medieval city of Assisi.

*HOTEL UMBRA*
*Owner: Alberto Laudenzi Family*
*Via degli Archi*
*06081 Assisi, Italy*
*tel: (075) 812 240   telex: 66122*
*27 rooms: Lire 60,000*
*Closed: mid-January to mid-March*
*Credit cards: All major*
*Central location off main square*
*About 177 km N of Rome*

The Hotel Florence is a moderately priced hotel in the charming ancient port of Bellagio. The location is prime - right on the main square. Across the street by the lake is a little tea terrace where you can have a snack while watching the boat traffic. If you are lucky enough to snare a front room with a balcony, you can step out through your French doors and be treated to a splendid view of Lake Como. There is a small reception area and, down a few steps, an intimate lounge with a fireplace, beamed ceiling and chairs set around tiny tables. A staircase leads to a guest dining room with a fireplace and ladderback chairs and to the guest rooms. On our last visit we were pleased to find many of the guest rooms have been redone - many with antique furnishings. Ours was a very cheerful, bright corner room with French doors opening onto a terrace where lounge chairs were invitingly set for viewing the lake. The hotel is owned by the Ketzlar family, who are real pros: the inn has been in their family for 150 years and is now managed by Mrs Freidl Ketzlar and her daughter, Roberta. They both speak excellent English and are extremely gracious. Bellagio is such an atmospheric little town that we are happy to be able to recommend a pleasant, well-run, moderately priced hotel.

*HOTEL FLORENCE*
*Owners: Ketzlar Family*
*22021 Bellagio (Lake Como)*
*Italy*
*tel: (031) 950 342*
*48 rooms: Lire 84,000 - 98,000*
*Open: April 25 to October 10*
*Credit cards: All major*
*Village center, near ferry*
*Lakefront location*
*Located 78 km N of Milan*

The Grand Hotel Villa Serbelloni is certainly appropriately named.    It definitely is GRAND.    In fact, the public rooms are almost overwhelming, with intricately painted ceilings, gold mirrors, fancy columns, Oriental rugs, gilded chairs, heavy chandeliers, and a sweeping marble staircase.    The bedrooms are quite nice, although I did not think the decor too outstanding.    However, the quality is superb: lovely percale sheets, soft down pillows, and large towels.    The service, too, is excellent.    Located in the gardens by the lake there is a large swimming pool.    If you prefer sightseeing or shopping to swimming, the colorful old port of Bellagio is just steps from the hotel.    If you tire of exploring the town of Bellagio, the ferry is only a few minutes away, or, if you want to be discreet, the concierge can arrange a special boat to pick you up at the private pier in front of the hotel.    Perhaps the original grandeur of the Grand Hotel Villa Serbelloni has faded a little, but if ornate elegance and the feeling of living in a masterpiece of a palace appeals to you, I think you will enjoy your stay here.    Pretend you are a guest at a weekend house party - given by royalty, of course.

*GRAND HOTEL VILLA SERBELLONI*
*Owner: Rudy Bucher*
*Manager: Giuseppe Spinelli*
*22021 Bellagio, Italy*
*tel: (031) 950 216 telex: 380330*
*82 rooms: Lire 295,000 - 575,000*
*Open: April 10 to October 10*
*Credit cards:  All major*
*Sumptuous palace on Lake Como*
*Swimming pool*
*Located 78 km N of Milan*

How lucky to find a "picture perfect" inn in the splendid ancient upper town of Bergamo (Citta Alta). And what a picture. The Hotel Agnello d'Oro sits just off the main Piazza Viejo, smugly facing its own tiny, intimate square, complete with tinkling fountain. The hotel, an olive drab with brown shutters and an awning in front, is tall and skinny - only two rooms wide but rising six stories high. An area of potted row-hedge defines the outdoor terrace. Inside, too, this old hotel is great. An ancient desk sits in the tiny lobby and to the right is a wonderful restaurant with crowds of copper, plenty of colorful old plates on the walls, cozy chairs and wooden tables covered with bright red and white checked tablecloths. The effect is cluttered but, oh, so gay. Upstairs the rooms are not for the fussy. They are very basic, but they are perfect for those on a budget whose love of romantic ambiance surpasses their desire for perfection in sleeping quarters. Even the fussy among you might adore waking up in the morning, opening the French doors, and stepping out onto your tiny balcony to greet the day. The front rooms are prime, with flower boxes on the iron railings. Another plus - although the government gives the Hotel Agnello d'Oro a third class rating, Michelin gives a two fork approval to the restaurant.

*AGNELLO D'ORO*
*Via Gombito, 22*
*24100 Bergamo (Citta Alta)*
*Italy*
*tel: (035) 249 883*
*25 rooms: Lire 52,500*
*Credit cards: AX, VS*
*Very basic small budget hotel*
*Marvelous walled medieval city*
*Located 47 km NE of Milan*

In 1550, King John of Portugal decided to give a little gift to the Emperor Ferdinand of Austria, so he purchased an elephant in India, shipped it to Genoa, then planned to "walk" it to Austria.   This giant beast grew weary about the time it reached Bressanone and was stabled for two weeks at the Am Hohen Feld Inn. Young and old came from miles around to see this impromptu "circus".   The proprietor of the Am Hohen Feld was obviously a master at marketing: to maintain the fame of his establishment, he promptly renamed his hotel - you guessed it - the "Elefant".   A picture of our friend the elephant was painted on the front of the building commemorating the sensational event.   But even without an elephant story this hotel is a winner.   Although the bedrooms themselves are a little drab, they are immaculately clean and comfortable.   In contrast to the simplicity of the bedrooms, the reception areas and dining rooms are fantastic, incorporating beautiful antiques, museum quality paintings and magnificent paneling, all of which are combined with great taste.   But, even if there were no elephant story nor an antique ambiance to the hotel, the Elefant would have another tremendous attribute: the food is fantastic.   Most of the eggs, butter, milk, fruit, and vegetables, and even the wine, come from the hotel's own farms.

*HOTEL ELEFANT*
*Owner: Hotel Elefant, Inc*
*Manager: Wolfgang Heiss*
*Via Rio Bianco, 4*
*39042 Bressanone, Italy*
*tel: (0472) 222 88  telex: 401277*
*45 rooms: Lire 172,000*
*Open: March to November 12*
*Swimming pool*
*NE Italy near Brenner Pass*
*Located 40 km N of Bolzano*

The Peralta is special - very special - not really a hotel at all, but rather a miniature medieval village tucked high in the coastal hills northeast of Pisa. This cluster of buildings had fallen into ruin when the famous Italian sculptress, Fiore de Henriquez, discovered the village, fell in love, and decided to bring the hamlet back to life. Fifteen years of reconstruction has resulted in a dream of a retreat. Fiore de Henriquez has her home and studio in one of the buildings - the others now house the few lucky guests who find their way to this secluded paradise. This hotel is definitely not for everyone. Those who like a slick hotel with the assurance that everything will always work perfectly had best find other accommodation. There are no promises here that there will never be a shortage of water or problems with the electrical power. But this is a small price to pay for those of you who love to walk through groves of chestnut trees, pick wildflowers along secluded paths, read a favorite book while soaking in the sunshine or, best yet, do absolutely nothing at all except enjoy the breathtaking view out over the valley to the sea. There is no planned activity at the hotel except for the camaraderie of fellow guests. However, if you want to do a little sightseeing, the Peralta is well located. Florence is only about 90 minutes away, Lucca (one of my favorite of Italy's walled cities) is about a half an hour's drive, Carrara (where Michelangelo came to hand-pick marble for his masterpieces) just a short excursion to the north and the seaside town of Viareggio close by. Although the concept of the Peralta is rustic, it far surpassed what I had expected. Although the rooms are simple, there is an elegance to their simplicity. Obviously the talents of Fiore de Henriquez were called upon in the design and decor - each room abounds with rustic charm, with extensive use of handmade tiles, what appear to be hand-loomed fabrics and attractive wooden beds and chests. Especially appealing is the tiny lounge where comfy sofas are grouped around a cozy fireplace. You will also be delighted to discover, tucked high on a tiny plateau above the hotel, a delightful pool with a terrace where guests can enjoy a splendid view to the sea.

Many of the guests are British - probably because all the space at the hotel is controlled by a travel agency in London. Most of the staff are also from Britain, and, I might add, those I met were exceptionally friendly and fun. The restaurant is closed on Thursdays so, except for breakfast, guests need to drive to one of the nearby towns for meals. Since it is also the staff's day off on Thursday, there are no arrivals scheduled for that day. Whatever day you do arrive, be sure you have a reservation. The hotel is really secluded and you will certainly not want to take a long drive only to discover the hotel is full - which it usually is. When you make your reservation, you will receive a map with directions on how to get to the Peralta. However, should you be arriving prior to receiving a map, this will help: drive to Camaiore (just north of Lucca) then watch for a sign to Pieve di Camaiore. You will wind up in the trees where occasionally you will spot, if you look carefully, a few handwritten signs to the Peralta, giving encouragement that you are not lost. Don't give up. Just keep driving as the road twists and becomes narrow and steep and then ends... at which point you park your car and continue on foot for the last quarter mile. (Leave you luggage in the car and someone will retrieve it for you later). I assure you the journey is worthwhile.

*PERALTA*
*Manager: Philip Harrison Stanton*
*Pieve Di Camaiore, Lucca, Italy*
*tel: (0584) 951230*
*14 rooms: Lire 83,000*
*Open: Easter to October*
*Credit cards: None*
*Res: Harrison Stanton & Haslam Ltd*
        *25 Studdridge St, London SW6 3SL*
        *tel: London (01) 736-5094*
*No children under 16*
*Swimming pool*
*Located 35 km NE of Pisa*

*Hotel Descriptions*

The Cenobio dei Dogi was formerly the summer home of the Genoese Doges, so it is no wonder that it has such an idyllic location nestled on a small hill which forms one end of Camogli's miniature half-moon bay. From the hotel terrace there is an enchanting view of the tiny cove lined with marvelous narrow old fishermen's cottages painted in all shades of ochres and siennas. The hotel has a very nice swimming pool, plus a private (though pebbly) beach. Many of the bedrooms have balconies which boast romantic views of this storybook scene. For tennis buffs, there is a tennis court, although I cannot imagine anyone wanting to play tennis with all the beautiful walking trails which make enticing spider web designs on the peninsula. Although the Cenobio dei Dogi is larger than most hotels which appear in this guide and its decor does not radiate antique ambiance, it possesses a solid, comfortable, no-nonsense kind of charm. It is not chic in the "jet set" style of hotels frequently found on the Riviera, but if you relate to gorgeous flower gardens, exceptional views, and slightly faded, "old world" comfort in one of the most picturesque villages in Italy, then I think you will love this hotel.

*HOTEL CENOBIO DEI DOGI*
*Manager: Mr Pasquini*
*Via Niccolo Cuneo, 34*
*16032 Camogli, Italy*
*tel: (0185) 770 041 telex: 211116*
*84 rooms: Lire 215,000 - 267,000*
*Credit cards: All major*
*Closed: January and February*
*Former summer Doges' palace*
*Pool, private beach, tennis*
*Near Portofino - Italian Riviera*
*Located 26 km SE of Genoa*

The Grand Hotel Quisisana conjures up the image of a Hollywood setting where the jet-set gather. The women, adorned in jewels and the latest swimming ensembles, sit in the sun and gossip about the latest scandal while their husbands (or boyfriends?) sit pool-side drinking Scotch and playing the game of grown boys - discussing their latest business ventures. But it is all great fun and quite in the mood of Capri which has been a playground for the wealthy since the time of the early Romans. The Grand Hotel Quisisana is a deluxe hotel with a gorgeous oval pool overlooking the blue Mediterranean. The air of formal elegance appears as soon as you enter the lobby decorated with marble floors, soft green velvet chairs, Oriental carpets, ornate statues, crystal chandeliers and beautiful paintings. All the bedrooms are well appointed and the deluxe rooms even have separate "his" and "hers" half-baths. Room rates include breakfast and lunch or dinner and you can choose from almost anything on the menu. The Grand Hotel Quisisana most definitely provides a setting and atmosphere to reflect the image of, and cater to, their jet-set clientele.

*GRAND HOTEL QUISISANA*
*Manager: G. Chervatin*
*Via Camerelle, 2*
*80073 Capri, Italy*
*tel: (081) 8370 7 telex: 710520*
*143 rooms: Lire 304,000 - 400,000*
*Open: April through October*
*Credit cards: All major*
*U.S. Rep: LHW*
*Rep tel: 800-223-6800*
*Beautiful pool in garden setting*
*Located on Island of Capri - near Naples*

The Hotel Luna savors one of the most beautiful locations on the Island of Capri. It is just a short walk from the main town yet, in atmosphere, it seems miles away from the bustle and noise. The hotel is perched on the cliffs overlooking the spectacular coastline of green hills that drop straight into the sea and from which emerge giant rock formations. There is an outside terrace for dining which captures this view, and the premium rooms have balconies overlooking the sea. There is a very large pool surrounded by flowers just a short stroll from the hotel which also has a splendid view. The decor of the hotel seems to be in need of refreshing. The overstuffed chairs and velvets and heavy furniture seem to conflict with the natural splendor of the landscape. However, the natural attributes are such that I think the hotel is definitely one of the best on Capri. The overall mood at the hotel is set by its delightful entrance. There is a covered trellis walkway which, in summer, is completely shaded by brilliant bougainvillea and grape vines and bordered by flowers. It is a wonderful introduction to the Hotel Luna and to what I am sure would make a lovely interlude by the sea.

*HOTEL LUNA*
*Via Matteotti, 3*
*80073 Capri, Italy*
*tel: (081) 8370433 telex: 721247*
*Open: April to October*
*48 rooms: Lire 127,000 - 248,000*
*Credit cards: All major*
*On cliff above the sea*
*Lovely views & lovely pool*
*Located on Island of Capri - near Naples*

If you are approaching Florence from the west, perhaps on your way from Milan to Florence, I highly recommend stopping en route, just before you reach Florence, at the Paggeria Medicca.  The hotel's address is Artimino, but the town is so small that I doubt you will find it on any map, so mark Carmignano instead on your map and when you arrive there you will find signs to Artimino, only a few minutes' drive farther on.  The hotel is cleverly incorporated into what were once the pages' quarters for the adjoining 16th-century Medicea villa "La Ferdinanda".  The long, narrow structure has been cleverly restored, preserving the many original chimneys which adorn the heavy, red-tiled roof.  An open corridor whose heavily beamed ceiling is supported by a stately row of columns forms a walkway in front of the rooms.  All of the guest rooms are simple, but very inviting, with tiled floors, pretty prints on the white walls, hand-loomed-looking white drapes hanging from wooden rods above the windows, and attractive antiques or copies of antiques as accents in each room.  There is a snack bar in the same wing as the hotel, but the main restaurant, Biagio Pignatti (which serves simple but delicious Italian cooking), is located in a nearby building which at one time housed the butler for the villa.  If you are a guest at the hotel, you have access to a delightful small Etruscan museum situated in the vaults of the adjoining Medicea villa "La Ferdinanda".

*PAGGERIA MEDICEA*
*Assistant Manager: Vania Pierini*
*Viale Papa Giovanni XXIII*
*50040 Artimino, Italy*
*tel: (055) 871 8081  telex: 571502*
*37 rooms: Lire 145,000*
*Open: All year*
*Credit cards: All major*
*Tennis courts (pool planned)*
*Located 20 km SW of Florence*

The Gaidello Club is unique in this guide series: this is the first time that an inn which cannot be booked on an individual basis has been included.  I did not know this when I first wrote to Paola Giovanna Bini (the owner) and, after stopping for lunch - with the best pasta I have *EVER* tasted, it was too late: my heart was won. So the Gaidello Club is included with the idea that frequently families or friends travel together making up their own small group (eight is the minimum number accepted at the inn).  Paola Giovanna Bini, who inherited the farm from her grandmother, assumed the awesome task of reconstructing the 250-year-old farm house and adding three apartments (suites) which have been restored and decorated with care, keeping in mind the original character of the country home. These suites vary in size, accommodating from two to five persons.  Although the rooms are pleasant, it is the food which makes this inn so very special: only the freshest vegetables and fruits are served; all the pasta is prepared the same day; the wines come from the farm's own vineyard; even the liqueur served after the meal is made from walnuts picked from the orchard.  However, Paola Bini wanted me to stress that it is *ABSOLUTELY NECESSARY* to make reservations for the restaurant which is open only for a minimum of eight to ten persons in order to justify the time needed in preparation of the food - all of which is strictly prepared the same day by hand.

*GAIDELLO CLUB*
*Owner: Paola Giovanna Bini*
*Via Gaidello, 22*
*Castelfranco Emilia, Italy*
*tel: (059) 926 806*
*3 suites: Lire 116,000*
*Only groups of 8 to 12 persons*
*Cooking classes can be arranged*
*Located about 26 km W of Bologna*

I visited the Pensione Salivolpi with the idea of including it only in our new guide featuring inexpensive places to stay. However, the hotel is so very pleasant, that for those of you looking for a "budget" hotel while roaming the Tuscany hills, we have included this small, attractive pensione. Although the address is Castellina in Chianti (in the heart of the famous Chianti wine region), you will actually find the hotel on the outskirts of town, on the left-hand side of the road leading from Castellina to the small town of Sant Donato. The old, weathered stone farmhouse sits almost on the road. It is only when you pull into the parking area that the lovely position of the inn is revealed - behind the main building there is a beautiful view terrace featuring a lovely large swimming pool. What a surprise to find such a wonderful addition to an inexpensive accommodation. The bedrooms are pleasant, reflecting the nice taste of the Salivolpi family who personally oversee the operation of their small hotel and will assist you with ideas for sightseeing excursions while exploring Tuscany. With Florence only 30 minutes north and Siena 15 minutes to the south, the Pensione Salivolpi provides a simple, but very pleasant, base of operation.

*PENSIONE SALIVOLPI*
*Owner: Etrusca Salivolpi*
*Via Fiorentina - Loc. Salivolpi*
*53011 Castellina in Chianti, Italy*
*tel: (0577) 740 484*
*19 rooms: Lire 55,000*
*Open: All year*
*Credit cards: None accepted*
*No restaurant*
*Swimming pool*
*Located 20 km N of Siena*

The Tenuta di Ricavo is unique.   It is not a "hotel" at all in the usual connotation, but rather a tiny village with peasants' cottages which have been transformed into delightful little guest rooms.   The stables are now the dining room and the barn is now the office.   You enter the parklike setting through a huge pine forest where small cottages are nestled in amongst the trees.   Gardens are everywhere and roses embellish the weathered stone cottages giving them a fairy-tale appearance. The total effect is absolutely enchanting.   Originally the village was the summer residence of a Swiss family who used it for holidays and later transformed it into an exquisite resort.   The family seeks no publicity.   They do not need it: the hotel is always filled with fortunate guests who have discovered this paradise.   However, this inn definitely is not for everyone.  It is quiet.  It is remote.  It is unstructured.   But it is a haven for the traveller for whom a good book, a walk through the forest, a swim in the pool, a drink at sunset with fellow guests, and a delicious dinner are fulfillment.

*TENUTA DI RICAVO*
*Owner: Lobrano-Scotoni Family*
*53011 Castellina in Chianti*
*Italy*
*tel: (577) 740 221*
*25 rooms: Lire 195,000 - 312,000 (includes 2 meals)*
*Open: April to mid-October*
*Credit cards: None accepted*
*Unique village hotel - 5 day minimum*
*Pool and 300-acre park*
*Hotel is comprised of small village*
*In the Tuscany Hills - S of Florence*
*Located 50 km S of Florence*

A book on the most charming hotels in Italy could not be complete without including one of the queens of the world, the Villa d'Este. Originally the hotel was a private villa built in 1568 by the Cardinal Tolomeo Gallio. He obviously had elegant (and expensive) taste, for the Villa d'Este is truly a fantasy land. From the moment you enter the enormous lobby with the sweeping staircase, marble, crystal, soaring ceilings, statues, and columns surround you. Everything is elaborate and ornate. Upstairs, the bedrooms are all very similar in decor with color-coordinated carpets, walls and bedspreads. Some of the bedrooms have prime locations overlooking the lake. Although the interior is beautiful it is the outside where the fun really begins. The hotel opens onto a large terrace where guests relax with refreshing drinks. Just a short distance beyond the terrace is the lake where there is a dock for boats and a very large swimming pool which extends out over the water. Across the road from the hotel there are beautiful tennis courts and within the nearby area are seven golf courses. However, the most stunning feature of the Villa d'Este is the park which surrounds it with lovely pathways winding between trees, a jogging course, glorious flowers, statues, and even a formal garden with a dramatic mosaic colonnade.

*VILLA D'ESTE*
*Manager: Mario Arrigo*
*22010 Cernobbio, Italy*
*tel: (031) 511 471 telex: 380025*
*180 rooms: Lire 438,000 - 521,000*
*Open: April to October*
*U.S. Rep: HRI, 800-223-6800*
*Credit cards: All major*
*Pool, tennis, squash and gym*
*Swimming, windsurfing, waterskiing*
*Located 53 km N of Milan*

The Anna Maria is located in Champoluc which is a small town almost at the end of the beautiful Ayas Valley which stretches north into the Alps almost to the Swiss border in northwest Italy. As you drive through the town of Champoluc you will see a small sign for the Anna Maria on the right side of the road just before you leave town. Turn right on this little lane which winds up the hill and you will see the Anna Maria on your right set in a serene pine grove. The Anna Maria is not a luxury hotel, but rather an old mountain chalet which is now a simple, but very charming, inn. There is a large deck for sunning which stretches across the entrance. Inside there is a lovely dining room - my favorite room - which exudes warmth and coziness with its wooden Alpine-style country chairs, wooden tables, and gay red checked curtains at the windows. Upstairs the bedrooms are not luxurious but most inviting, with wooden paneling on the walls and a rustic ambiance, and best of all - every bedroom has a private bathroom. Perhaps the most winning feature is Anna Maria, the owner, who is your hostess and oversees her little inn with a gracious charm. The atmosphere is "homey" - not for the fussy but wonderful for those who love the friendliness of a country inn in a mountain village.

*ANNA MARIA*
*Owner: Anna Maria*
*11020 Champoluc, Italy*
*tel: (0125) 307 128*
*25 rooms: Lire 75,000 - 107,000*
*Excellent value*
*Open: Jul through Aug & Dec through mid-Apr*
*Chalet style - lovely setting*
*Mountain location - NW Italy*
*Located 175 km NW of Milan*

The Ca'Peo, a well known restaurant serving some of the finest food in Italy, is located high in the coastal hills south of Genoa. You might think you will never arrive as the road winds ever upward through groves of olive and chestnut trees. But the way is well signposted, and just about the time you might be ready to despair, you will find a wonderful old farmhouse, owned by Franco Solari, who is host and in charge of the wines, and his wife, Melly, who is the chef. As we checked in, the entire family was in the kitchen busily chopping vegetables, rolling out pastry and preparing the fish for the evening meal. The dining room, enclosed on three sides by large arched windows, takes advantage of a sweeping view to the sea. Fabulous food is definitely the main feature: however, in a modern annex there are five suites available for guests who want to spend the night. The decor here is not antique, but each of the large suites is pleasant, and after lingering over a wonderful meal accompanied by delicious wines, how nice to walk just a few steps to your bed. A final note: the Ca'Peo is only about half an hour's drive from the popular resort of Portofino, so you might want to stay here instead or at least treat yourself to a memorable meal - but call ahead, reservations are always needed.

*CA'PEO*
*Owners: Franco & Melly Solari*
*Via dei Caduti, 80*
*16040 Chiavari a Leivi, Genoa, Italy*
*tel: (0185) 319 090*
*5 suites: Lire 120,000*
*Closed: November & December*
*Restaurant closed on Mondays*
*Credit cards: VS*
*Famous "restaurant with rooms"*
*Located 44 km SE of Genoa*

I was puzzled to receive a hotel questionnaire response postmarked St Simon's Island, Georgia.    But quickly all was explained.    It was from James Adams who had been living in Europe, perfecting his Italian cooking skills at one of the finest restaurant-hotels in Italy, the Locanda del Sant'Uffizio - Ristorante da Beppe. The owner, Giuseppe Firato ("Beppe"), speaks no English so when our request for information arrived, he asked his American protege to respond.    After visiting the hotel, I can only say that it was more perfect than anticipated.    Below is Jamie's wonderful letter describing so superbly his "home away from home".

"Originally in the 1500s the Locanda del Sant'Uffizio was a Benedictine monastery and served as such up until the mid 1800s after which time it passed into private hands serving as a farm.    In 1972, Signore Giuseppe Firato (Beppe), a man from the village, bought the farm and slowly began converting it into its present form. Naturally at first there were only several rooms while the rest of the buildings were used for farming and wine growing.    Through the years rooms have been added very carefully, with great respect for the traditional aesthetics, and now there are 35 guest rooms.    All furnishings are antique and every detail of the decor has been rigorously overseen personally by Signore Beppe and his wife, Carla, with the result being a very tasteful, elegant, yet relaxed hotel cozily nestled amongst the vineyards in the hills of Monferrato.    Other features include a tennis court, a swimming pool (in front of which one can have breakfast and lunch in the warm months) and, last but not least, there is the Ristorante da Beppe, an exquisite restaurant serving the finest of Piemontese cuisine.    It is of course owned and operated by the Firato family, and, in fact, the restaurant preceded the hotel.    It has earned one Michelin star and has been rated highly in notable Italian guides such as Espresso and Veronelli.    When one combines the charm and relaxation of this elegant hotel with the pleasures of such a refined table, one is left with a very memorable experience."

I cannot resist adding a few more words - there are so many features that make the Locanda del Sant'Uffizio very special. Without a doubt, the Firato family is responsible for the ambiance of warmth and hospitality which radiates throughout the hotel. Signore Beppe was born in the tiny village (population 50) where the hotel is located. When his father who owned a small bar died, Signore Beppe took over - although he was only a boy at the time. The rest is history: the bar grew into a restaurant, the restaurant into a tiny hotel, the small hotel into a delightful resort. Such a success story is not surprising when you meet Signore Beppe. He speaks no English. He does not need to. His charismatic charm transcends all language barriers. It is no wonder his restaurant - isolated in the countryside - is filled each night with chicly dressed Italian clientele: Beppe greets each of them with an exuberant warmth, and the food is outstanding, truly a gourmet delight. Also, excellent wines are served, most of which are produced from grapes grown on the property and matured in large oak vats in the winery adjacent to the hotel. The price of the dinner is expensive (but for a 6 course meal with wines included - a bargain). In closing I would like to add that James Adams, a most charming young man, is soon returning to the United States to open a restaurant (probably in New York) featuring the style of cooking he has learned during his year of living in Italy. It will be a huge success, I am sure, and in our next Italian edition I will give you the address. Note: you will not find Cioccaro di Penango on your map so just locate the town of Moncalvo - the hotel is 5 kilometers south.

*LOCANDA DEL SANT'UFFIZIO*
*RISTORANTE DA BEPPE*
*Owner: Giuseppe Firato*
*14030 Cioccaro di Penango, Italy*
*tel: (041) 91 271*
*35 rooms: Lire 125,000*
*Closed: January and August 10 to 20*
*Credit cards: All major*
*Swimming pool, tennis*
*90 km E of Turin, N of Asti*

The Hotel Menardi dates back 200 years. Originally it was a peasant's farmhouse, but as Cortina's popularity as a fabulous ski center has spread so has the town, and now the farm is located right on the outskirts of town on the main road heading north. Nevertheless, the Menardi family, who have owned the home for a century and a half, have managed to maintain the country flavor through the use of many antiques, marvelous old prints on the walls, old clocks, giant dowry chests, Oriental carpets, and beautiful hanging cupboards - all set off by the warmth and gaiety of flowers everywhere. The bedrooms vary in decor but are all pleasant and with private bath. A chalet behind the hotel plus a deluxe addition that is being built will increase the number of bedrooms. It seems that the Menardi farm just naturally evolved into a hotel. At first it gave shelter to the men carting loads over the Cimabanche Pass who needed a place to sleep - more often than not in the hay loft. Today the inn is a simple but wonderful small hotel whose special ingredient is the old-fashioned warmth and hospitality of the gracious Menardis.

*HOTEL MENARDI*
*Owner: Menardi Family*
*112 Via Majon*
*32043 Cortina D'Ampezzo*
*Italy*
*tel: (0436) 2400*
*40 rooms: Lire 136,000 - 210,000 (includes 2 meals)*
*Open: Jul-Sep, late Dec-Mar*
*Old farmhouse - many antiques*
*In the Dolomites - NE Italy*
*Located 133 km E of Bolzano*

The Castello di Pomerio dates from the 9th century and has been restored with exquisite taste and quality. As you roam the antique-filled rooms, you will be aware of the impact of their perfection that is everywhere. Each detail of restoration shows loving care: in fact, even ancient frescoes have been meticulously restored. Some of the bedrooms are in the main castle and others are in a wing across the road that is cleverly connected to the castle by a tunnel so that you still feel a part of the main hotel. All of the bedrooms vary in decor, but all are outstanding. Most of the ones I saw had wonderful wooden beds and attractive heavy curtains; many had cozy fireplaces ... all had charm. For the exercise enthusiast, there is a tennis court plus both an indoor and an outdoor swimming pool. Through the ages, this hotel has changed hands many times. At one point, its past even included use as a silk factory. How lucky for the tourist, though, that Lital Magni Donati now owns the hotel and has turned it into a masterpiece of romantic lure where one can stop for a few days and live like a king in his "own" castle.

*HOTEL CASTELLO DI POMERIO*
*Owner: Lital Magni Donati*
*Via Como, 5*
*22036 Pomerio di Erba, Italy*
*tel: (031) 611 516 telex: 380463*
*58 rooms: Lire 230,000 - 300,000*
*Credit cards: All major*
*Sauna, inside & outside pools, tennis court*
*Near Lake Como*
*Located 44 km N of Milan*

The Badia Montescalari, an 11th-century abbey, was recommended to me by an Italian hotelier who said it is "the most chic place to stay in all the countryside around Florence".    I cannot judge if it is the most chic, but there is no doubt that it is a fascinating hotel blessed with a sensational location.    The road winds up through a rather dense forest for over 2 kilometers until the hotel is reached, sitting in secluded splendor high in the Tuscany hills.    Its history as an abbey appears as you enter the hotel through an inner courtyard.    The lounges and office are on the first level from which one staircase leads up to the 10 guest rooms and another leads down a wide set of stone steps to the kitchen and dining room.    The owners of this very special hotel are two gentlemen from Florence who specialize in renovating buildings with great respect for maintaining the original ambiance. They have done a beautiful job here - staying at the Badia Montescalari is like stepping back into history.    The bedrooms vary, but all abound with excellent antiques.    Guest rooms 1, 2, 3 and 4 are the most spacious and have private bathrooms en suite.    The dining room is a showplace - with intricate vaulted ceilings and a massive open fireplace.    Another plus: horses are available for guests who like to ride.

*BADIA MONTESCALARI*
*Owners: Paolo Ignesti & Andrea Antoniazzi*
*Via Montescalari, 129*
*Figline Vald'Arno*
*tel: (055) 059 596*
*10 rooms: Lire 240,000, includes dinner*
*Closed: February*
*Credit Cards: None accepted*
*Not suitable for children*
*Beautiful secluded castle*
*Located 37 km S of Florence*

The Punta Est is a lovely old villa perched on a hilltop overlooking the sea. When the home was converted to a villa an annex was added to provide more bedrooms. However, it still gives the friendly feeling of a private home. This warmth of reception and attention to detail is the result of the management of the Podesta family who own and manage the inn. They seem dedicated to making your stay as enjoyable as possible - even their German Shepherd seems to want to welcome you. There are little terraces with lovely views snuggled at various levels among the trees and on one of these terraces is a swimming pool. There is also access to the public beach of Finale Ligure which can easily be reached by walking down the path to the main highway and following the tunnel beneath the highway to the beach. The rooms in the main villa are smaller and more old-fashioned than those in the newer annex which are more reminiscent of an American motel. There is a small dining room for breakfast which is especially inviting with its blue and white English bone china service. This is just one example of a very nice touch offered by owners who really want to please.

*HOTEL PUNTA EST*
*Owner: Podesta Family*
*17024 Finale Ligure, Italy*
*tel: (019) 600 611*
*40 rooms: Lire 130,000 - 135,000*
*Open: May 15 to September 20*
*Credit cards: AX VS*
*Hilltop villa overlooking sea*
*Pool and access to the beach*
*Italian Riviera W of Genoa*
*Located 72 km W of Genoa*

The Grand Hotel Villa Cora is a mansion, originally built during the 19th century by the Baron Oppenheim as a gift for his beautiful young bride.  Among the many romantic tales of the Villa Cora is the one about Oppenheim's wife who, so the story goes, became enamored of one of her many admirers.  The jealous baron was so enraged that he threatened to burn the entire mansion.  Luckily for you and me, he was stopped in time from this mad endeavor by his friends, and today this magnificent villa is a stunning hotel.  Although only about a five-minute taxi ride from the center of Florence (or a half an hour walk), the Grand Hotel Villa Cora is eons away in atmosphere.  You feel more like a guest on a country estate rather than in a city hotel.  The villa is set in intricate gardens and even has a pool.  The interior of the hotel is very ornate and sumptuous.  You can almost hear the sounds of laughter and music drifting through the gardens, and indeed the mansion has always been famous for its dramatic parties: at one time the villa was the residence of Napoleon's wife, Empress Eugenia, whose gay entertaining was the talk of Florence.  Now this grand palace-like home can be yours for days of dreams and romance.

*GRAND HOTEL VILLA CORA*
*Manager: Valerio Rastrelli*
*Viale Machiavelli, 18/20*
*50125 Florence, Italy*
*tel: (055) 229 8451 telex: 570 604*
*56 rooms: Lire 426,000*
*Open: All year*
*Credit cards: All major*
*Sumptuous villa - parklike setting*
*Swimming pool in a lovely garden*
*Located 20-minute walk from heart of Florence*

On our last research trip to Italy we stayed at the Loggiato Dei Serviti in Florence. What a refreshingly pleasant experience. Many of the hotels in Florence are lovely, but fabulously expensive: others are reasonably priced but shabby and dark. So it was an exceedingly happy surprise to find a light, airy, antique-filled small hotel - at an extremely reasonable rate. The Loggiato dei Serviti has only recently opened, so perhaps that is why the prices are so excellent for the value received - there are plans to add another 11 rooms soon, and also to add more amenities such as direct dial phones, piped music, hair dryers, TVs and mini-bars. I am afraid that the prices might mushroom with the improvements - I hope not. In the meantime, although this is not a deluxe hotel, I think you will be very pleased. There is a small reception area as you enter, beyond which is an intimate little bar where snacks are served (there is no restaurant at the hotel). A miniature elevator - just large enough for two people to squeeze into - takes you upstairs to the spacious bedrooms, each with private bath and each decorated individually with antiques. If friends or family are travelling, there are two suites, one of which even has two bedrooms and two bathrooms. Again, these suites are excellent values - and most attractive.

*LOGGIATO DEI SERVITI*
*Owners: Budini Tattai Sons*
*Piazza S.S. Annunziata, 3*
*50122 Florence, Italy*
*tel: (055) 263592 or 219165*
*19 rooms: Lire 130,500*
*Open: All year*
*Credit cards: All major*
*Antique-filled small hotel*
*Located in the heart of Florence*

The Lungarno Hotel is superbly located directly on the Arno River and only a few minutes' walk from the Ponte Vecchio. Although most of the hotel is of new construction, the architect cleverly incorporated an ancient stone tower into the hotel so it is easy to rationalize including this hotel - one of my favorites in Florence - into this travel guide. The interior of the hotel is traditional rather than antique in decor, but the decorating is done with excellent taste and the effect is most pleasing. Lovely soft colors are used throughout with beautiful prints and many fresh flowers. The bedrooms are very comfortable and those who book well in advance can request one of the rooms overlooking the Arno. Those who really plan ahead might even be lucky enough to secure one of the few rooms with a balcony overlooking the river. What a treat to sit on your own little balcony in the evening and watch the Arno fade into gold and the Ponte Vecchio glow in the setting sun. There are several rooms in the tower itself, one of which is especially romantic with its remaining old stone wall and its staircase that leads up to a little balcony and a third bed. Several of the other rooms in the new portion of the hotel also have balconies which can be used as sleeping alcoves.

*LUNGARNO HOTEL*
*Manager: Nedo Naldini*
*Borgo San Jacopo, 14*
*50125 Florence, Italy*
*tel: (055) 264 211 telex: 570129*
*66 rooms: Lire 231,000 - 341,000*
*Open: All year*
*Credit cards: All major*
*Some rooms with view terraces*
*Short walk to Ponte Vecchio*
*Located on the Arno*

Once in a while a hotel stands out like a beacon amongst its competition. The Monna Lisa, located about a five-minute walk from the heart of Florence, is just such a hotel. Recently the Italian government changed the rating of the Monna Lisa from a pension to a four star hotel, but by any standards this is an appealing small hotel. The entrance is nondescript but hides a small inn blooming with charm. The present owner is a descendant of Giovanni Dupre, the famous sculptor, which perhaps accounts for some of the art treasures. Also found in the hotel are many superb and elegantly displayed antiques, many of which are family heirlooms. The hotel has only 28 rooms, which are always occupied. I was able to see only one of the rooms, but the one I saw was delightful with exquisite antique beds and a beamed ceiling. Some of the guest rooms have balconies overlooking a charming garden. I cannot describe the others, and the manager said that each one is different; however, with the excellent taste shown in the lounges and dining room, I imagine that all of the rooms are pleasing. The Monna Lisa, at one time, was an elegant Renaissance palace and you will certainly feel like nobility when you are her guest.

*HOTEL MONNA LISA*
*Owner: Ciardi-Dupre Family*
*Manager: Riccardo Sardei*
*Borgo Pinti, 27*
*50121 Florence, Italy*
*tel: (055) 247 9751 telex: 573 300*
*28 rooms: Lire 150,000 - 190,000*
*Open: All year*
*Credit cards: All major*
*Exceptionally delightful small inn*
*5-minute walk from heart of Florence*

The Regency is located on a small parklike square only a ten-minute walk from the heart of Florence. It is, however, a world away in atmosphere - instead of the noise of motorcycles and the bustle of tourist-filled streets, you have a peaceful, quiet, elegant setting. The mood of being "away from it all" is enhanced as you enter the hotel. Again you are protected: the front door is usually kept locked and only guests of the hotel are allowed inside. You ring the front door bell just as you would in a private home. Although small, the Regency is a deluxe hotel and, in fact, it is quite amazing that with only 36 rooms the Regency can offer so many of the luxuries that are usually found only in larger hotels, such as a concierge to assist you with any of your personal needs and an intimate restaurant in a gorgeous wood paneled dining room. A larger restaurant will soon be open in an adjoining townhouse. The bedrooms are spacious and luxurious, with excellent lighting and elegant bathrooms. I would prefer a few more antiques, but these are found mostly in the lounges and the dining room. At the present time, the Regency spreads into several adjacent "homes" with a garden connecting the wings.

*HOTEL REGENCY*
*Owner: Amedeo Ottaviani*
*Piazza Massimo d'Azeglio, 3*
*50121 Florence, Italy*
*tel: (55) 245 247 telex: 571058*
*36 rooms: Lire 435,000*
*Open: All year*
*Credit cards: All major*
*U.S. Rep: David B. Mitchell*
*Rep tel: 800-372-1323*
*Quiet, elegant "home-like" hotel*
*10-minute walk to heart of Florence*

As an alternative to staying in downtown Florence, you might want to consider instead the Villa La Massa which is located on the banks of the Arno about a 15-minute drive from town.   The Villa La Massa is actually composed of three buildings - each old and each having its own unique charm.   This beautiful estate originally belonged to the rich and powerful Giraldi family: inscribed tombstones, underground tunnels and a chapel still remain from this period of the villa's ancient history.   Although the Villa La Massa is very old, the hotel offers all of the modern amenities including tennis courts, a swimming pool, air conditioning, refrigerators in the guest rooms and a choice of restaurants.   One of the restaurants, the Fusica, is very elegant and located in what used to be the dungeon.  The other, the Candele, is light and airy and has a beautiful terrace for outdoor dining.  If you have a car, then the Villa La Massa might make an appealing alternative to staying in the heart of Florence: especially in summer when you can do your sightseeing during the day and return to a pool and garden setting at night.

*HOTEL VILLA LA MASSA*
*Manager: C. Manetti*
*50010 Candeli*
*Florence*
*Italy*
*tel: (55) 630051 telex: 573555*
*40 rooms: Lire 277,000 - 455,000*
*Credit cards: All major*
*Located on bend of Arno River*
*Swimming pool, tennis courts*
*Located 7 km E of Florence*

The Bencista is a gem. A real "find" for the traveller who wants a congenial, appealing, family run hotel near Florence which has charm and yet is reasonably priced. This delightful old villa, romantically nestled in the foothills overlooking Florence, is owned and managed by the Simoni family who are always about, personally seeing to every need of their guests. Simone Simoni speaks excellent English, and on the day of my arrival he was patiently engrossed in conversation with one of the guests, giving him tips for sightseeing. Downstairs there are a jumble of rooms, each nicely decorated with rather dark, Victorian furniture. Upstairs are the bedrooms which vary in size, location, and furnishings. Some are far superior to others; however, they are all divided into only two price categories: with or without private bathroom. Many people return year after year to "their own" favorite room. During the season, reservations are usually given only to guests who plan to spend several days at the hotel - this is an easy requirement because the hotel is beautifully located for sightseeing in both Florence and Tuscany. (If you do not have a car, there is a bus at the top of the road which runs regularly into Florence.) Two meals (breakfast and lunch or dinner) are included in the price and there is an excellent kitchen serving simple, good Italian cooking. One of the outstanding features of the pensione is its view - there is a splendid terrace where guests can enjoy a sweeping panorama of Florence.

*PENSION BENCISTA*
*Owner: Simone Simoni*
*50014 Fiesole (Florence), Italy*
*tel: (055) 59 163*
*35 rooms: Lire 140,000 (includes 2 meals)*
*Credit cards: None accepted*
*Lovely old villa - beautiful views*
*On hillside overlooking Florence*
*Located 8 km NE of Florence*

It would be difficult to find another hotel with as many attributes as the Villa San Michele. In fact, almost impossible. How could one surpass a wooded hillside setting overlooking Florence, a stunning view, gorgeous antiques, impeccable management, gourmet dining, and, as if this were not enough, a building designed by Michelangelo. The Villa San Michele was originally a monastery whose inner courtyard dates back to the 15th century. No expense has been spared in the reconstruction of this fabulous building to maintain the ancient ambiance. There are only 28 guest rooms, and, although not large, they are decorated with elegant taste. The lounges, dining rooms, terraces and gardens are also exquisite. Breakfast and either dinner or lunch are compulsory, but this is no problem since the food is delicious. Meals can be enjoyed either in a beautiful dining room or on a lovely veranda which stretches along the entire length of the building. A swimming pool has recently been built on a secluded little terrace above the hotel, and, as with every feature of the Villa San Michele, it is beautiful, perfectly situated to capture the view and surrounded by fragrant gardens.

*VILLA SAN MICHELE*
*Manager: Maurizio Sacconi*
*Via Doccia, 4, Fiesole*
*50014 Florence, Italy*
*tel: (055) 59451 telex: 570643*
*28 rooms: Lire 600,000 - 1,240,000 (includes 2 meals)*
*Open: mid-March to mid-November*
*U.S. Rep: LHW*
*Rep tel: 800-223-6800*
*Credit cards: All major*
*Swimming pool*
*Luxury hotel in hills above Florence*
*Located 7 km NE of Florence*

The Hotel Villa del Sogno is located at Lake Garda, not lakefront, but instead perched on a hillside overlooking the lake. I am not sure of the history of the villa, but apparently it was an estate - obviously of a family of means, for the hotel is a prime piece of property. A small private road winds up the hill through a grove of trees until the villa is spotted, a traditional ochre-colored, red-tiled-roof building set off with white trim and green shutters. As you enter the hotel, it is as if you were in a private home. A large wooden, open staircase leads to the upper floors where the spacious bedrooms are attractively decorated in traditional style furniture. The choice rooms of course are those in the front with a view of the lake. One of the very finest features of the Villa del Sogno is its especially large terrace in the back of the hotel which has a majestic view out over the trees to the lake. The day I visited, many of the guests were enjoying afternoon tea as they savored the view from the comfort of lounge chairs. Another favorite retreat is the swimming pool which is tucked onto a terrace nestled to the side of the hotel. The grounds surrounding the pool are quite lovely, with potted plants placed strategically about the various levels of parklike grounds giving color and fragrance to the air.

*HOTEL VILLA DEL SOGNO*
*25083 Fasano di Gardone Riviera*
*Italy*
*tel: (0365) 20228*
*47 Rooms: Lire 150,000*
*Open: April to mid October*
*Credit cards: All major*
*Beautiful lake view*
*Swimming pool*
*2 km NE of Gardone Riviera*
*Located 129 km E of Milan*

I was enchanted with the Villa Fiordaliso (a fetching pink and white villa superbly located on the shore of Lake Garda) when I spent the night in one of its antique-filled bedrooms overlooking the lake several years ago. At that time, I wrote a glowing description of this beautiful little hotel, only to learn from the manager that I was one of the last guests - the villa was closing to the public. Nevertheless, when researching for our latest edition, I went by the Villa Fiordaliso "for old times' sake" and, to my delight, found it open again. The emphasis now is definitely on the dining. Luckily, however, seven bedrooms are again offered: each is unique in decor, yet all have every modern comfort plus stylish pieces of furniture, inlaid parquet flooring, engraved golden ceilings, marbles and alabasters. The rooms facing the lake have a lovely view, and are quieter since they are away from the noise of the street. For history buffs, the villa offers a bit of romance - the Villa Fiordaliso was a gift of Mussolini to his mistress, Claretta Petacci. In fact, Claretta's own bedroom is one of the rooms available and is a real winner with an enormous marble bathroom.

*VILLA FIORDALISO*
*Owner: Pierantonio Ambrosi*
*Manager: Stefano Sganzerla*
*Via Zanardelli, 132*
*25083 Gardone Riviera, Italy*
*tel: (0365) 201 58  telex: Fiorda 301088*
*7 rooms: Lire 128,000*
*Open: Mar through Oct & Dec 15 to Jan 1*
*Credit Cards: AX VS DC*
*Romantic lakefront villa*
*Located 130 km E of Milan*

When we first saw the Pensione Giulia it was rated by the government as a third class pensione.   However, the hotel is no longer a simple pensione.   On our last visit we were pleased to note that all the rooms now have a private bathroom and even a swimming pool has been built into the garden.   The inn is a superb old Victorian-style villa in a large park which extends down to Lake Garda.   A dramatic staircase at the end of the hallway leads to the simple bedrooms.   In addition to the rooms in the main villa, guest rooms are available in a modern annex.   On the same level as the entrance hall is a dining room which is quite appealing with enormous chandeliers and antique-style chairs.   On a lower level, opening out onto the garden, is another dining room which is quite modern and lacking in charm.   When the weather is warm, the favorite place to dine is on the terrace where tables are set to enjoy the sun and a view of the lake.   Wherever you choose to dine, you will enjoy good home-style Italian cooking - it is not surprising that the food is well prepared since Signora Bombardelli, the owner, is usually bustling about in the kitchen personally overseeing the preparation of the next meal.   She does not speak much English, but is extremely gracious and is always about seeing that her guests are happy.   Not fancy, the Pensione Giulia offers a very pleasant stay at reasonable prices with a superb lakefront location.

*PENSIONE GIULIA*
*Owner: Bombardelli Family*
*25084 Gargnano, Lake Garda, Italy*
*tel: (0365) 71022*
*16 rooms: Lire 82,000 - 87,000*
*Open: April to October*
*Credit cards: MC*
*Swimming pool*
*On the western shore of Lake Garda*
*Located 141 km E of Milan*

The Villa Fiorio is located about 15 miles south of Rome near the hilltown of Frascati which has always been a favorite playground of the Romans. It might be an especially good choice of a hotel if you are flying into Rome and do not want to drive too far your first day. The villa sits on the main highway which runs between Frascati and Grottaferrata, but although the street is right in front of the hotel, there are gardens to either side of it and a lovely lawn with trees in the rear. Among the olive trees to the right of the hotel is a beautiful large swimming pool. Here you can enjoy a country ambiance very close to Rome but at a fraction of the Rome hotel prices. The Villa Fiorio was built as a summer home for a wealthy Italian doctor and the interior is quite ornate with fancy Italian furniture, lots of mirrors, gilded tables, and elaborate wall sconces. Upstairs the bedrooms continue the ornate motif. In the reception hall there are slides of the various bedrooms showing each unique decor so that if space is available, you can choose the room that most appeals to your particular taste.

*VILLA FIORIO*
*Owner: Pierino Maccari*
*Viale Susmet, 25*
*00046 Grottaferrata, Italy*
*tel: (06) 945 9276*
*20 rooms: Lire 130,000*
*Open: All year*
*Credit cards: All major*
*Old villa set in garden*
*Beautiful swimming pool*
*Located 21 km S of Rome*

The Villa La Principessa is a lovely old mansion surrounded by beautiful gardens. In a parklike setting behind the hotel is a large swimming pool with lounge chairs and umbrellas for relaxing in the sun. In the distance are lush, green hills. The entire effect is refreshing and serene. Unfortunately the interior of the villa does not maintain the same degree of quiet elegance as does the exterior. The entry hall has some lovely antiques and a beautifully paneled ceiling, but the carpet is a loud plaid which would be better suited for a Scottish castle. In one of the lounge rooms, the carpet is purple and the walls and draperies a bright green. The bedrooms, too, are decorated in bright colors. The dining room, however, tones down and is quite charming. This is an expensive, well maintained, luxury hotel. Although the decor is rather bright, I think those of you looking for a stopover near Pisa will find this definitely the best choice.

*HOTEL VILLA LA PRINCIPESSA*
*Manager: Giancarlo Mugnani*
*55050 Massa Pisana*
*Lucca, Italy*
*tel: (0583) 370 037 telex: 590068*
*44 rooms: Lire 210,000 - 325,000*
*Closed: December to late February*
*Credit cards: All major*
*U.S. Rep: David B. Mitchell*
*Rep tel: 800-372-1323*
*On the road between Pisa and Lucca*
*Located 19 km N of Pisa*

The Hotel Santavenere was a wonderful surprise.   I had seen pictures of the hotel before I arrived and it looked rather like a motel - a long, narrow building with each floor a row of guest rooms.   The photographs did not do it justice - the hotel is absolutely a knockout.   From the moment you walk into the lobby, the gracious ambiance of an exquisite country home surrounds you.   The living room is elegant, but not "stuffy" - soft, comfortable sofas and lounge chairs slipcovered in an attractive country print form cozy conversation nooks.   Excellent antiques lend further charm.   Plus, there are many nautical accents, such as delightful models of sailboats, giving even more interest to the room.   The dining room follows in excellent taste - a large, airy room with highbacked wooden chairs, fresh flowers on the tables, and white linen cloths.   The bedrooms are beautifully decorated with excellent copies of antiques and have modern bathrooms.   Each bedroom opens onto its own terrace or balcony with lovely sea views.   The location too is exceptional: the back of the hotel drops down a steep wooded hillside, but there is a beautiful green lawn adorned with a swimming pool which stretches to the side of the hotel.   Beyond the lawn the cliffs drop suddenly to the sea and a small private pier.

*HOTEL SANTAVENERE*
*85040 Maratea*
*Italy*
*tel: (0973) 876 160*
*44 rooms: * Lire 165,000*
*\* Rate includes 2 meals*
*Open: June to September 26*
*Credit cards: VS AX DC*
*On the sea, pool, tennis*
*Located 220 km S of Naples*

*Hotel Descriptions*

Once in a while a hotel is so perfect that it is tempting not to include it - selfishly fearful that if everyone knows how exceptional it is there might not be "room in the inn" when we return. The Castel Freiberg is just that special, but conscience dictates sharing with you our Shangri-La. This fantasy castle cresting a hilltop in the mountains near Merano exudes charm. All of the public rooms are a decorator's dream where priceless antiques abound. The bedrooms, each individual in decor, are all tastefully furnished and some have balconies overlooking the mountains. Even if the setting were not perfect, this castle would be a "winner" because of its enchanting decor, but add to this a gorgeous restaurant in a richly paneled room with gourmet cooking, and what else could you possibly desire? Well, there is more. If you talk to the masterful and professional concierge, Wolters Siegrid, you will find that surrounding the Castel Freiberg is a maze of splendid walking paths. Also, of course, there is a beautiful pool in a garden setting with the Dolomites as a dramatic backdrop, as well as an inside pool, clay tennis courts, an exercise room, and more - you must go to see for yourself.

*HOTEL CASTEL FREIBERG*
*Owner: Bortolotti Family*
*39012 Merano, Italy*
*tel: (0473) 441 96 telex: 401081*
*27 rooms: Lire 240,000 - 260,000*
*Open: Easter to October*
*Credit cards: AX DC MC*
*U.S. Rep: David B. Mitchell*
*Rep tel: 800-372-1323*
*2 pools, tennis, children's play yard*
*In the countryside 7 km S of Merano*
*Located 28 km W of Bolzano*

Schloss Labers is a lovely old castle which dates back to the 11th century. It has a picturesque setting on a hillside surrounded by vineyards and overlooking the beautiful Adige Valley which is framed by dramatic mountains. Although not luxurious, this castle has character and charm. Probably its major attribute is excellent management by the Stapf-Neubert family who oversee every detail of the operation and take personal responsibility to insure that everyone is properly pampered. I spoke to Mr. Neubert who told me that his grandfather came from Copenhagen in 1885 and bought the castle which became so popular with his visiting friends that it soon became a prosperous hotel. The lounges and dining rooms are not fancy, but have a lived-in, comfortable ambiance. The central staircase dramatically leads upstairs where there are 35 bedrooms - many with lovely mountain views. The setting of this old castle is peaceful and quiet, and if you enjoy being in the countryside, you will delight in the marvelous network of walking paths leading in every direction.

*HOTEL CASTEL LABERS*
*Owner: Stapf-Neubert Family*
*Via Labers, 25*
*39012 Merano, Italy*
*tel: (0473) 344 84*
*35 rooms: Lire 140,000*
*Open: end March to November*
*Credit cards: AX DC MC*
*Overlooks valley and mountains*
*Swimming pool, good for families*
*Mountains in Northern Italy*
*Located 28 km W of Bolzano*

If you love picturesque chalet-style hotels in quiet, isolated surroundings, then the Hotel Vigiljoch will definitely be your cup of tea.   There is absolutely no highway noise: there are no cars.   The only way to reach the hotel is by cable car which you take from the town of Lana which is near Merano in the mountains of northeastern Italy.   The cable car rises quickly from the floor of the valley and has a breathtaking view of the vineyards and apple orchards.   When the cable car reaches the tip and slowly joggles into the terminal you will see the Hotel Vigiljoch just to the left of the station.   In summer, flowers will be bursting from every window and umbrellas will be gaily decorating the front terrace.   Inside you will find quite simple bedrooms, but many of which have balconies with a sweeping view of valley and mountain.   The bedrooms are small but pleasantly furnished with furniture painted in an Alpine motif.   A sprinkling of antiques highlights the lounges.   My very favorite room is an intimate, wood-paneled dining room whose wonderful country prints of blue and red mingle with delightful, light wooden furniture.

*HOTEL VIGILJOCH*
*1-39011 Vigiljoch*
*Lana bei Merano, Italy*
*tel: (0473) 512 36*
*Open: Jun to Oct and Dec 20 to Apr 20*
*41 rooms: Lire 80,000*
*Credit cards: None accepted*
*Pool, mountaintop setting*
*Accessible only by cable car*
*Near Merano in Northern Italy*
*Located 24 km W of Bolzano*

As I sit looking out the window of my room, savoring the sweet morning air drifting through the window and viewing a breathtaking vista of rolling hills dotted with classic Tuscany villas, I almost do not want to write about Le Colombe. It is too perfect. It is so special that I want to keep it secret. However, sharing is our business and so I write and hope that only those of you who will appreciate the very unique qualities of this tiny inn will find your way here. Le Colombe (romantically meaning "the Dove") is owned by Carmen and Francesco Forlando. Francesco is a true professional, having been in the hotel business since he was a boy of 16. Through the years his ability and gracious charm led him to the very top: he has been manager of some of the finest hotels in the world, including the Hotel San Domenico in Taormina and the Villa San Michele in Fiesole (Florence). It was while overseeing the Villa San Michele that Francesco and his lovely Mexican wife, Carmen, began looking for a perfect country home. They found it. Just 23 kilometers south of Florence they discovered a farmhouse nestled amongst groves of olive trees and fields of vines. They bought the property, and with absolute perfection, they have refurbished this simple, 12th-century farmhouse into a dream. Francesco attributes the perfection in the decor to Carmen - if so, her taste is faultless. From the moment you enter the vine-covered, stone building, the ambiance is one of elegant country charm. The living room abounds with antiques but the mood of comfort is set by sofas covered in floral print fabric, grouped in front of a large fireplace. The living room flows into the dining room, also filled with antiques. But, without a doubt, my favorite room in the house is the kitchen-family room. Here a superb, very old country dining room table sits in the middle of the room, surrounded by wooden chairs, each with a comfy cushion, whose blue and white fabric ties in with the provincial blue print wallpaper. The room is dominated by a massive fireplace which is accented by pewter plates, baskets of all sizes and shapes and sprays of fragrant herbs hanging to dry. The family room flows into the country kitchen where heavy beams, white walls, baskets of fresh vegetables, and white and blue tiles complete the appealing scene. Stairs lead from the family room to the upper floor where only three rooms are available, each with its own bathroom. The guest rooms are not large. They are not deluxe. But they are perfect. Each is different, exuding its own personality. Wonderful antiques are used throughout, while exquisite linens, hand-embroidered towels, fresh flowers, extremely comfortable beds, and windows opening out to views of the entrancing Tuscany landscape make each room special. You will definitely feel like a guest (Francesco kept stressing to me that Le Colombe is *NOT* a hotel, but rather "a home with rooms"). Indeed you will feel like a guest as you sit on the veranda, sharing an evening drink with the other guests and enjoying the fields stretching out before you bathed in the captivating Tuscany mellow light. Guiermo, Carmen's comical dog, is usually stretched out listening to the conversation and several kittens nap in the sun close by. Breakfast (a splendid traditional "English breakfast") is the only meal served, but your hosts will tell you of many excellent choices within a short driving distance. Also, they will share with you wonderful tips on where to go each day, not only to the obvious attractions such as Siena, Assisi and San Gimignano, but to their own favorite "finds": gems of walled villages, excellent wineries, local markets, and wonderfully priced shopping. If you enjoy peace and quiet, Le Colombe would make a perfect choice for a place to stay instead of Florence - you could enjoy country-style living yet be only half an hour from the city.

*LE COLOMBE*
*Owners: Carmen & Francesco Forlando*
*Via della Mandria, 2*
*50024 Mercatale Val di Pesa*
*(Firenze), Italy*
*tel: (055) 82 12 29*
*3 rooms: Lire 140,000*
*Open: April 1 to October 31*
*Credit cards: None accepted*
*Located 23 km S of Florence*

The Antica Locanda Solferino, once an old tavern, is an excellent choice if you are looking for a simple, small hotel that is moderately priced. Here you will receive great value, for this is a very pleasant, tiny hotel charging rates that are most reasonable in the very expensive city of Milan. The location is good too - on a tiny street near the Piazza della Republica, within walking distance of most of Milan's attractions. The hotel's main claim to fame is its restaurant of the same name which serves delicious food in a delightful, cozy dining room. (Even if you do not stay at the hotel, you might want to stop by for a meal.) A small desk in the lobby serves both the dinner clientele and also the hotel guests. From the reception area stairs lead to the upper level where 11 rooms are tucked away. Each room, although small, reflects excellent taste. The room I saw had a wonderful antique wooden bed and was appealingly furnished in an "old-world" style. Because all of the rooms were occupied, I was able to see only one room, but the manager told me that although all are individually decorated, they are very similar in ambiance. On my last visit to Milan I had hoped to stay at the Antica Locanda Solferino, but, although I called several months prior to my arrival, the hotel was fully occupied. This was actually no surprise since the hotel is very popular. But be forewarned: if you want accommodation, plan far in advance.

*ANTICA LOCANDA SOLFERINO*
*Manager: Curzio Castelli*
*Via Castelfidardo, 2*
*20121 Milan, Italy*
*tel: (02) 659 9886*
*11 rooms: Lire 112,600*
*Open: All year*
*Credit cards: None accepted*
*Located near center of Milan*

The Hotel Gran Duca di York is tucked on a tiny street just a few blocks away from the Piazza del Duomo. It is not surprising that it is so close to the spectacular Duomo (cathedral) since its original purpose was as a residence for some of the priests, including the Cardinal of Milan, Pio IX, who later became Pope. The hotel is a mustard yellow building with an arched balcony above the main entrance. The lobby is spacious with two large marble columns framing the entrance, large oil paintings decorating the walls and a suit of armor standing in quiet grandeur at the end of the room. The reception area is the only part of the hotel that smacks of "old-worlde" ambiance: the rest of the hotel is decorated in simple, sometimes a bit stuffy, furnishings. In a city where most of the moderately priced hotels have no charm, the Gran Duca di York makes a good choice. A final note: the hotel is almost impossible to find. The short street where it is located is frequently not shown on any of the city maps. I consider myself an expert "finder" and I became hopelessly lost. Your best bet is to ask the hotel to send you their map, but if this is not possible, ask for directions at the tourist office located in the Piazza del Duomo - from there it is only a short walk to the hotel.

*HOTEL GRAN DUCA DI YORK*
*Manager: Mario Visentini*
*Via Moneta, 1/a*
*Piazza Cordusio*
*20123 Milan, Italy*
*tel: (02) 876 563 or 874 943*
*33 rooms: Lire 143,000*
*Closed: August*
*Credit cards: None accepted*
*No restaurant*
*Located short walk from the cathedral*

We were so disappointed when our favorite hotel in Milan, the Hotel Alla Scala, closed. So we made a trip to Milan to find a replacement for those of you who want a hotel beautifully located in the old section of the city, within minutes of the cathedral, the theater and the shopping. After looking at many hotels, the Grand Hotel et de Milan most closely fills the bill. The mood is set as you enter into a small, dignified reception area with a beautiful wood paneled registration desk, Oriental rug set on cool marble floors, and flowers and plants adding a bit of color. Beyond the lobby is a very large lounge, light and airy from a glass skylight ceiling, with an ornate carved marble fireplace the center of attention. Through arched doorways you enter a small bar. My favorite room, however, is the intimate little nook next to the bar: here the walls are covered in large murals which accentuate the five small round tables where guests may sit and order light meals. The bedrooms are comfortable, but have rather drab, somewhat dated, modern decor.

*GRAND HOTEL ET DE MILAN*
*Manager: Gian Piero Guarnori*
*Via Manzoni, 29*
*20121 Milan, Italy*
*tel: (02) 801 231 telex: 334505*
*89 rooms: Lire 396,000*
*Open: All year*
*Credit cards: All major*
*Located in heart of Milan*

Of course, it is fun to be in the heart of Venice, but for half the price of what you would pay for a first class hotel there, you can stay twenty minutes to the north at the Villa Condulmer, a splendid 17th-century villa whose rooms more closely resemble a museum than a hotel.  The rooms are grand, with fabulous wall frescoes painted by Moretti Laresi.  The eight rooms in the original villa are the most sumptuous in decor: however, in the heat of summer you might prefer the newer wing whose rooms provide the option of air conditioning.  There are several lovely dining rooms for you to enjoy.  In addition, when the weather is balmy, you may choose to have your meals served outdoors on the terrace.  In the garden is a large pool and nearby a gym set which would appeal to children.  For adult "play", there is a golf course adjacent to the hotel where arrangements can be made for you to play if you have a letter of introduction from your club in the United States. Should you like horseback riding this too can be arranged.

*VILLA CONDULMER*
*1021 Mogliano Veneto,*
*Italy*
*tel: (041) 457 100*
*33 rooms: Lire 175,000*
*Open: April to October*
*Credit cards: AX DC MC*
*Pool, tennis, play yard*
*Good stopover for children*
*About 4 km NE of Mogliano Veneto*
*Located 18 km N of Venice*

The Castello di Gargonza is not a traditional hotel at all, but rather a romantic walled, storybook village, surrounded by forests and perched at the crest of a hill. The 900-year-old complex of stone buildings now receives guests. Nineteen of the picturesque farmhouses are available by the week. Most have one or two bedrooms plus a kitchenette and many also have a fireplace - perfect for chilly evenings. Each small cottage is named and when you make a reservation, the hotel will send you a map of the town and a description and a sketch of each of the houses so that you can choose what most appeals to your needs. In addition to the "housekeeping" houses, there are also seven regular guest rooms. The village oozes with charm: staying here is like stepping back to medieval times. However, the decor leaves something to be desired, with an extensive use of plastic furniture interspersed with more traditional pieces. However, the overall ambiance is terrific and the hotel is a fabulous bargain, especially for two couples travelling together or families with children who want a homebase for exploring Tuscany. Note: although the address is the town of Monte San Savino, the hotel is actually located about 8 kilometers west, on road 73 to Siena.

*CASTELLO DI GARGONZA*
*Owner: Count Roberto Guicciardini*
*Azienda Castello di Gargonza*
*52048 Monte San Savino Arezzo, Italy*
*tel: (0575) 847021  telex: 571466 Redco I*
*7 Rooms: Lire 135,000 (3 day minimum)*
*19 Houses: from Lire 650,000 weekly*
*  (week minimum)*
*Open: Easter through December*
*Credit Cards: AX*
*Walled hilltop castle*
*Located 35 km E of Siena*

The town of Orvieto, just off the main expressway between Rome and Florence, is one of the most picturesque of all the Umbrian hilltowns. The small city crowns the top of a hill - an intriguing sight which can be viewed from miles away. Less than a 10-minute drive south of Orvieto is a 12th-century Gothic abbey which has been converted into a hotel. Here you can stay surrounded by the romantic ruins of yesteryear. We have overnighted at La Badia, enjoying the pool and the "old-world" atmosphere, and readers have written that they too liked their visit. But we continue to receive letters complaining of the miserable attitude and surly service of the personnel - so be forewarned. We are still including La Badia (with reservations) because the town is so outstanding, but unless the management becomes more cordial, we will have to drop it. The hotel itself is nice: the dining room is especially attractive with an enormous, high vaulted stone ceiling, wrought iron fixtures, heavy wooden beams, eye-catching copper accents and, at one end, a cavernous fireplace complete with a spit for roasting. The bedrooms are not large, but are comfortable and many have a stunning view of the town of Orvieto. In the meadows behind the monastery there is a pool which makes a welcome respite from a day on the road.

*LA BADIA*
*Owner: Count Giuseppe Fiume*
*05019 Orvieto Scalo, Italy*
*tel: (0763) 90 359*
*24 rooms: Lire 189,000 - 320,000*
*Credit cards: All major*
*Hotel built into ancient abbey*
*Pool, tennis, good for children*
*About 5 km S of Orvieto*
*Located 115 km N of Rome*

Lo Spedalicchio is an old medieval fortress which has been restored and brought back to its original role of sheltering travellers.  It is located only about a 10-minute drive from Siena, in the center of Ospedalicchio di Bastia.   The town itself holds no charm, but the hotel is attractive and shows taste throughout in its decor. There is convenient parking in front of the hotel from which it is only a few steps into a very large reception area.  A lounge opens off to the left with sofas and chairs upholstered in a deep-blue fabric which contrasts nicely with the old stone walls and the high vaulted ceilings.   The dining room is spacious with many tables and moderns chairs, giving the impression that the hotel perhaps is used for groups or large functions.   Upstairs the bedrooms are quite attractive - all reflecting the mood of the old castle with tiled floors, heavy off-white drapes hanging from wooden rods, antique (or reproduction of antique) furniture, and bedspreads which appear to be made from hand-loomed fabric.  The castle is just off the main highway between Florence and Assisi so is conveniently located for an overnight stop.

*LO SPEDALICCHIO*
*Manager: Mrs Giancarla Costarelli*
*Piazza Bruno Buozzi, 3*
*06080 Ospedalicchio di Bastia, Italy*
*tel: (075) 809323*
*25 rooms:  Lire 80,000*
*Open: All year*
*Credit Cards: VS DC AX*
*Ten minute drive from Siena*
*14th-century castle*
*Located: 170 km N of Rome*

The Villa Le Barone was once the home of the famous Tuscan family, Della Robbia, whose delightful terra cottas are still seen throughout Italy. Most of the estate now has been beautifully converted into a deluxe small hotel, but the present owner, Duchessa Franca Viviani Della Robbia, still maintains a charming vine covered cottage for her own use. Although she is now in her eighties, the Duchessa comes frequently to the villa to insure that her impeccable standards and exquisite taste prevail. Staying at the Villa le Barone is very much like being the fortunate guest in a private, elegant home set in the gorgeous Tuscany hills. There are only 25 guest rooms, all of which vary in size and decor, but each with an individual charm. In addition, there is a lovely pool on a terrace overlooking the vineyards and out to the mellow hills beyond. Wonderful little terraces are found secluded in the park-like setting where guests can find a quiet nook to read or just to sit and soak in the beauty. The food is divine and in balmy weather lunch can be taken in the garden and dinner perhaps inside in a charming dining room which formerly housed the stables. Reservations are accepted for a minumum of three nights, but that should be no problem - three nights will be too short an interlude to spend in this romantic paradise.

*VILLA LE BARONE*
*Owner: Duchessa Franca Viviani Della Robbia*
*Manager: Caterina Buonamici*
*Via San Leolino, 19*
*50020 Panzano in Chianti, Italy*
*tel: (55) 852 215*
*25 rooms: Lire 260,00 - 300,000 (includes 2 meals)*
*Minimum stay 3 days*
*Open: Easter through October*
*Villa in the Tuscany hills*
*Located 31 km S of Florence*

Our first introduction to La Scuderia was one idyllic evening when we sat outside in the garden with friends enjoying an absolutely simple, yet superb dinner.    Perhaps the magic was the balmy air, the delicate wine or just the delicous homecooked meal - but it was truly a memorable event.    The little restaurant is owned and operated by Stella Casolato and her beautiful daughter, Monica.    Stella stays busy in the kitchen while Monica serves the tables with a gracious, gentle efficiency.    It was not until I revisited the restaurant the following day that I realized that a few rooms are also available.    I had expected to find spotlessly clean, nice rooms - but what a surprise to discover that, although extremely reasonable, the rooms are charming with accents of antiques.    There are only three guests rooms which share a very large, beautifully kept bathroom down the hall.    In addition there is a suite with its own private bath - a wonderful bargain for families or friends travelling together.    Although this is a simple inn, it is extremely appealing and the warmth of Stella and Monica should make this a wonderful choice for those looking for an inexpensive base for exploring the Chianti wine region.

*LA SCUDERIA*
*Owners: Stella & Monica Casolato*
*Badia a Passignagno*
*Sambuca Val di Pesa, Italy*
*tel: (055) 807 1623*
*3 rooms sharing one bathroom:  Lire 45,000*
*1 suite with private bath: Lire 350,000 week*
*Open: All year*
*Restaurant closed Wednesdays*
*Credit cards: None accepted*
*Beautiful little restaurant with rooms*
*Located 32 km S of Florence*

How smug I felt at "discovering" the Castel Pergine, for here is a picturebook castle perfect for the budget minded tourist.   No need to forfeit romance and glamor for even though the Castel Pergine is inexpensive, it has a fabulous location dominating a hilltop above the town of Pergine.   Luckily, this castle has been delightfully transformed into a small hotel with incredible views out over the valleys and wooded hills.   From the tower you can even see two small lakes in the distance inviting a picnic.   The Castel Pergine is far more famous as a restaurant than a hotel (Michelin gives the kitchen a two fork rating.)   The dining room has a wonderful medieval decor, gorgeous views, and delicious food.   There are, however, a few simple bedrooms.   The ones I saw were somewhat camp-like with basic beds, a wash basin, and a chest of drawers.   None of the rooms had private bathrooms, although there are, of course, facilities on each floor.   But for the price conscious the total ambiance of this castle in the sky is worthy of any budget itinerary - especially if you are with children who will love their personal Disneyland-like castle.

*CASTEL PERGINE*
*Owner: Fontanari Family*
*38057 Pergine, Italy*
*tel: (461) 531 158*
*12 rooms: Lire 60,000 - 80,000*
*Open: May through October*
*Ancient castle - lovely views*
*Excellent for children*
*Hilltop castle - 2.5  km E of Pergine*
*Located 152 km NW of Venice*

I am such a romantic that, as the boat chugged across the lake from Stresa to the medieval fishing village of Isola dei Pescatori and I saw the Hotel Verbano with its reddish-brown walls, dark green shutters, and tables set on the terrace overlooking the lake, my heart was won - completely.   The lobby is a bit shabby with its rather lumpy and worn furniture; however, the room then opens onto a very nice dining room whose arched windows overlook Lake Maggiore.   A second dining area is set up on the terrace with romantic views of the lake.   Upstairs the twelve bedrooms vary considerably.   One I saw was quite drab but another was very charming with hand painted furniture.   The views from some of the bedrooms are very nice. The Hotel Verbano has a marvelous restaurant.   When we first visited, the same cook had been creating meals for 28 years.   Unfortunately, she is now gone, but the owners wrote that they still have an excellent kitchen featuring wonderful home-style Italian cuisine and freshly caught fish from the lake.   This is not a hotel for those who want everything "perfect", but for those who love a romantic setting at a reasonable price, this special small hotel has great appeal.

*HOTEL VERBANO*
*Owner: Zacchera Family*
*28049 Isola dei Pescatori, Stresa*
*Borromee Isole, Lake Maggiore, Italy*
*tel: (0323) 30408 telex: 200269*
*12 rooms: Lire 96,000*
*Open: Mid-April through October*
*Credit cards: VS AX DC*
*Lovely lakefront restaurant*
*Island in Lake Maggiore*
*Located 80 km NW of Milan*

The Relais El Toula is a tiny, eight-room, super deluxe, exquisite inn located less than an hour's drive north of Venice.   Just to be included in the elegant "Relais et Chateaux" hotel association almost automatically means a divine hotel.   The Relais El Toula is not only a member of this prestigious family of hotels, but is also rated one of their most deluxe hotels in Italy.   The villa has an idyllic, country setting.   The original villa is flanked by two arcaded wings which stretch to the sides giving the building an elegant, long, low image.   After driving through the vineyards you arrive at an iron gate through which you enter into a courtyard and the hotel.   Inside there is an abundance of fresh flowers in the lounges and delightful bedrooms.   In addition to the lovely park-like setting and the beautiful rooms, there is another bonus - the food and wines are superb.   It is not surprising that the hotel is so exceptional, for it is owned by Alfredo Beltrame, a real pro in the inn-keeping profession.   He is the founder of the Toula hotel chain.

*RELAIS EL TOULA*
*Director: Giorgio Zamuner*
*Via Postumia, 63*
*31050 Ponzano, Treviso, Italy*
*tel: (0422) 969023  telex: 433029*
*8 rooms:  Lire 300,000 - 360,000*
*Credit cards: AX DC*
*U.S. Rep: David B. Mitchell*
*Rep tel: 800-372-1323*
*Lovely villa, own vineyards, pool*
*Located 35 km N of Venice*

The Il Pellicano has been beautifully designed in the traditional villa style and, although not old, looks as though it has snuggled on the hillside overlooking the Mediterranean for many years. The facade is of stucco, painted a typical Italian russet and set off by a heavily tiled roof. Vines enwrap the building, further softening its effect. One enters the bright lobby whose white walls, wooden beamed ceilings, gay sofas, antique accents, and enormous displays of fresh flowers enliven every conceivable nook and cranny. The overall impression is one of light and color - and great taste. Beyond the reception area is an outdoor dining terrace. As the terrace extends down the hillside, there is a beautiful pool romantically perched at the cliff's edge. From the pool a staircase leads to a pier at the water's edge. Along this path, small individual terraces with lounge chairs and mats for sunning have been built into the rocks. In front of the hotel is a tennis court, again surrounded by flowers.

*IL PELLICANO*
*Managers: Ennio & Nadia Emili*
*58018 Porto Ercole, Italy*
*tel: (0564) 833 801   telex: 500131*
*31 rooms: Lire 220,000 - 520,000*
*Credit cards: AX DC*
*U.S. Rep: David B. Mitchell*
*Rep tel: 800-372-1323*
*Superb cliff-top view location*
*Tennis, swimming pool, ocean swimming*
*Located 160 km N of Rome*

Many years ago I stayed at the Piccolo Hotel - and liked it very much.   However, we did not include it in our guide until now because it is quite basic and is on the busy road that leads into town.   This time, with hotel rates becoming so incredibly high in Portofino, we decided to include it as the best choice for anyone who wants to stay here without spending a fortune.   The Piccolo sits just above the road, on the right-hand side, as you drive into the village.   The appearance is of a small villa, which indeed I am sure it used to be.   The reception area used to be the entrance hall beyond which is a lounge area and then the dining room.   Stretching across the front is a balcony where tables are set for snacks and lounging, a favorite spot for guests, especially on warm days.   Downstairs there are accents of antiques which give a homey ambiance to an otherwise modern feel.   The bedrooms are upstairs and are basic in decor although some have French doors opening out to pretty little wrought iron balconies.   A flight of steps up from the hotel leads to a pleasant path which winds through the trees to the center of Portofino, surely one of the most colorful fishing villages in Italy.

*PICCOLO HOTEL*
*Owner: Bezzi Family*
*Via Duca degli Abruzzi, 31*
*16034 Portofino, Italy*
*tel: (185) 69015*
*26 rooms - Lire 100,000 - 114,000*
*Open: March through November*
*Credit cards: None accepted*
*Located 22 km E of Genoa*

The Splendido is truly a luxury hotel. Located up a winding, wooded road high above the town of Portofino, it sits majestically above the beautiful blue Mediterranean and overlooks the boats which are moored in Portofino's lovely harbor. The hotel is much like a very stately, wealthy country home. On a terrace below the hotel is an enormous swimming pool. There is also a tennis court located in the gardens to the left of the hotel. The public rooms are charming with comfortable chairs covered with floral prints and fresh flowers galore. There is a delightful outdoor terrace where meals are served. The bedrooms too are lovely and many have balconies which overlook the sea. There are also romantic little pathways originating from the hotel. You can stroll the wooded grounds and stop along the way at strategically placed benches to enjoy incomparable views. The Splendido is deluxe and expensive, but it is a beautiful hotel. If you love luxury and desire a resort setting in one of the most naturally scenic parts of Italy, you will certainly enjoy the marvelous Splendido.

*HOTEL SPLENDIDO*
*Manager: Antonio Marson*
*16034 Portofino, Italy*
*tel: (0185) 69551 telex: 331057*
*52 rooms: Lire 701,000 (includes 2 meals)*
*Credit cards: All major*
*Closed: October 28 to March 28*
*Beautiful swimming pool, tennis*
*Hilltop setting above Portofino*
*Located 35 km E of Genoa*

The Albergo Casa Albertina is a prime example of what a difference management can make.   There is a wide choice of hotels in the picturesque little fishing village of Positano -  many, like the Casa Albertina, with spectacular views, many with pleasant decor, many with good meals.   However, they don't have Michele Cinque who is an outstandingly gracious, warmhearted hotelier - nothing seems too much trouble to make each guest feel very special.   It is not surprising that Michele is such a pro - he has been in the hotel business for many years, having been the manager of one of Positano's most deluxe hotels (Le Sirenuse) before deciding to spend full time helping his wife and mother-in-law manage the Casa Albertina. The hotel is really a family operation: Michele is usually at the front desk ready to care for the guests, his mother-in-law is in charge of the kitchen while his wife helps out wherever needed.   Two sons are also working at the hotel and one of them has already taken over its official management - and quite ably, I might add.   The hotel (which is built into a 12th-century house) clings to the hillside above Positano, a position which affords superlative views, but also means a strenuous walk into town. However, you might never want to stray from the lovely terrace or the quiet of your room where you can savor the panorama of colorful Positano from your own balcony.

*ALBERGO CASA ALBERTINA*
*Manager: Michele Cinque*
*Via Tavolozza, 4*
*84017 Positano, Italy*
*tel: (089) 875 143*
*21 rooms:  Lire 180,000 (includes 2 meals)*
*Open:: All year*
*Credit cards: DC AX EC*
*Beautiful views from all of the rooms*
*Located 55 km S of Naples*

Le Sirenuse is a superb luxury hotel tucked smack in the middle of the picturesque ancient fishing village of Positano.   It is no wonder that so many writers and artists have been attracted to this colorful town of brightly hued houses clinging to the precipitous hillside as it drops down to its own small bay.   And it is also no wonder that so many of these men of fame have found their way to the oasis of Le Sirenuse. From the moment you enter the hotel lobby the mood is set with fresh white walls, tiled floors, oil paintings on the walls, and accents of antiques.   The hotel cascades down the hill and so almost all the rooms capture a wonderful view out over the quaint rooftops and the tiled domed cathedral to the shimmering blue waters of the bay.   It is only a short walk through the perpendicular streets until you are on the beach.   The dining room has walls of glass which allow the maximum enjoyment of the vista below, but most diners prefer the splendor of eating outdoors where the deck is set with tables for dining.   On another level of the hotel there is a small pool for sunning and dipping.

*LE SIRENUSE HOTEL*
*Manager: Luigi Bozza*
*Via C. Colombo, 30*
*84017 Positano, Italy*
*tel: (089) 875 066 telex: 770 066*
*60 rooms: Lire 364,000 - 470,000*
*Open: All year*
*Credit cards: All major*
*U.S. Rep: LHW*
*Rep tel: 800-223-6800*
*Swimming pool, delightful views*
*Old fishing village on Amalfi Drive*
*Located 55 km S of Naples*

The Il San Pietro di Positano is touted as one of the most delightful deluxe hotels in the world. It is. There is no question about it. From the moment you approach the hotel "class" is evident: no large signs; no gaudy advertising; just an ancient chapel along the road indicates to the knowledgeable that an oasis is below the hill. After parking in the designated area near the road, you take an elevator which whisks you down to the lounge and lobby. You walk out of the elevator to a dream world - an open spacious world of sparkling white walls, tiled floors, colorful lounge chairs, Oriental rugs, antique chests, flowers absolutely everywhere, and arches of glass through which vistas of greenery and sea appear. To the right is a bar and to the left is a marvelous dining room - again with windows of glass opening to the view, but with the outdoors appearing to come in, with the walls and ceilings covered with plants and vines. The bedrooms too seem to be almost a Hollywood creation - more walls of glass, bathrooms with views to the sea, and balconies on which to sit and dream. If you can tear yourself away from your oasis of a bedroom, an elevator will whisk you down the remainder of the cliff to the small terrace at the water's edge. If all this sounds gaudy, it isn't. It is perfect.

*IL SAN PIETRO DI POSITANO*
*Owners: Salvatore & Virginia Attanasio*
*84017 Positano, Italy*
*tel: (89) 875 455 telex: 770072*
*60 rooms: Lire 350,000 - 450,000*
*Closed: December to March 14*
*Credit cards: all major*
*U.S. Rep: E&M, 800-223-9832*
*Just south of Positano on Amalfi Drive*
*Located 58 km S of Naples*

For those who want to be smack in the middle of the colorful fishing village of Positano, the Palazzo Murat might be just your cup of tea.   It is superbly located - surrounded by shops and only steps down to the beach.   The hotel consists of two parts: the original building (a 200-year-old palace) plus a new wing which stretches out as an extension to the side.   The new section is a standard hotel - pleasant but not unusual.   However, the palace is quite special, with a faded-pink patina whose charm is accented by wonderful arched alcoves, intricately designed windows and magenta bougainvillea clinging to the walls and cascading from the wrought iron balconies.   The entrance to the hotel is through a sun-drenched patio, a favorite gathering spot for guests.   Within, the "old-world" feeling is maintained with tiled floors, white walls and formal settings of antique sofas and chairs.   Upstairs, in the palace section, are five bedrooms, some with wonderful French doors opening onto small balconies which capture a view of the bay.   The rooms in the original building have no air conditioning, but the walls are so thick they supposedly form their own insulation against the heat.   The only meal served is breakfast: this is actually a bonus since there are so many quaint restaurants in Positano enticingly nearby.   At the time we visited the hotel, plans were being made to upgrade it into a higher category - if this has happened the price might unfortunately have increased significantly from what is shown below.

*HOTEL PALAZZO MURAT*
*Owners: Attanasio Family*
*Via dei Mulini, 23*
*84017 Positano, Italy*
*tel: (089) 875 177*
*30 rooms: Lire 125,000 - 130,000*
*Open: Easter to October 15*
*Near the beach - heart of Positano*
*Located on Amalfi Drive 55 km S of Naples*

The Relais Fattoria Vignale is a very polished, sophisticated small hotel located in the heart of the Chianti wine region in the small town of Radda. The hotel has recently opened in what was the manor house of one of the large wine estates where the family's wines are still produced and are readily available in a winery shop across the street. The hotel is located right on the main street near the center of town, but nevertheless there is a country atmosphere because the back of the hotel opens up to lovely views of rolling hills striped with vineyards and dotted with olive trees. Capturing this idyllic view is a large swimming pool with comfortable lounge chairs along the side. Inside, the rooms are all beautifully decorated with a combination of authentic antiques and excellent reproductions. Care has been taken in the restoration to preserve many of the nice architectural features of the manor such as heavy beams, arched hallways, decorative fireplaces, and painted ceilings. One of the most appealing of the rooms is an antique library where guests are welcome to browse.

*RELAIS FATTORIA VIGNALE*
*Via Pianigiani, 15*
*53017 Radda in Chianti*
*Italy*
*tel: (0577) 738 300*
*23 rooms: Lire 128,000 - 192,000*
*Open: April through October*
*Credit cards: AX*
*Originally an 18th-century farm*
*In the heart of Chianti wine region*
*Located 52 km S of Florence, 31 km N of Siena*

It is no wonder that the Hotel Caruso Belvedere has such an especially spectacular site in Ravello - it was built as a palace in the 11th century by a noble family who probably had their pick of real estate.   The views of the rugged Amalfi coast from the dining terrace perched high in the clouds is gorgeous.   Many of the bedrooms too have vistas.   Although the decor is rather drab, the views just can't be surpassed.   If you choose the Caruso Belvedere, splurge and ask for one of their most deluxe rooms.   These are simply decorated without much style *BUT* they have enormous balconies which stretch the width of the room to capture again the incredibly romantic coast below.   You will wake in the morning to the sound of birds and the scent of flowers intermixed with the fragrance of the vineyards which drifts up from the terraces beneath your balcony.   The Hotel Caruso has more to offer than just its marvelous views.   The dining room offers excellent food including a divine specialty of the house - a delicious chocolate souffle which will linger in your memory perhaps as long as the view.   The meals are accompanied by wines from their own vineyards.

*HOTEL CARUSO BELVEDERE*
*Owner: Caruso Family*
*Via Toro, 52*
*84010 Ravello*
*Italy*
*tel: (089) 857 111*
*26 rooms: * Lire 142,000 - 174,000*
*\* Rate includes 2 meals*
*Credit cards: AX*
*Hilltown above Amalfi Coast*
*Located 66 km S of Naples*

The Marmorata Hotel is cleverly converted from the shell of an old paper mill. Only a few of the old paper mills are still in operation, but at one time the Amalfi area was famous for its production of fine paper. The official address of the Marmorata Hotel is Ravello: however, it is not located in the cliff town of Ravello, but rather on the coastal highway. As you are driving north from Salerno to Ravello you will see the sign to the hotel which is snuggled in the rocky cliffs between the road and the sea. As you enter the hotel you notice the nautical theme carried throughout the decor from the chairs in the dining room to the mirrors on the walls. The interior is charming with comfortable leather lounge chairs and small Oriental rugs. There is a lovely terrace plus, on a lower level, snuggled into the rocks, a small swimming pool. The bedrooms are small, but nicely decorated, again with the seafaring motif: the beds seem to be built into captains' sea chests and nautical prints are on the walls. The bathrooms are also small, but modern and attractive. All of the bedrooms have radios, color televisions, telephones, air conditioning and small refrigerators. Many of the rooms have an excellent view of the water and rugged coast.

*MARMORATA HOTEL*
*Owner: Camera d'Afflitto Family*
*Strada Statale, 163*
*84010 Ravello, Italy*
*tel: (089) 877 777 telex: 720667*
*40 rooms: Lire 140,000 - 190,000*
*Credit cards: VS DC AX*
*Pool, small pier, waterfront*
*Lovely views from bedrooms*
*On the coast below Ravello*
*Located 64 km S of Naples*

There is something magical about the Hotel Palumbo, a 12th-century palace now one of the most special hotels in Italy owned since 1875 by the charming Vuilleumier family. The location is perfect - up in the clouds overlooking the terraced vineyards and beyond to the brilliant blue sea which dances in and out of the jagged rocky coast. The Palumbo is a divine small hotel. The romance begins when you enter the beautiful lobby with its ancient atrium of arched colonnades, green plants flowing from every nook, masses of fresh flowers and beautiful antiques. Each small corner is an oasis of tranquility from the intimate bar to the cozy antique filled tiny lounges. There is a beautiful dining room with a crystal chandelier, bentwood chairs and a fireplace, but usually meals are served on the breathtaking terrace which perches like a bird's nest in the sky. Wherever you dine, the food is superb and the elegantly gracious owner, Pasquale Vuilleumier, frequently pauses at each table - an attentive host seeing to the contentment of each guest. There is a charming garden in the rear with a vine covered terrace overlooking the Amalfi coast. Another tiny patio which captures both the sun and the view is tucked onto the roof of the villa. There are only 20 bedrooms, each individually decorated and appealing with its own personality. A few guest rooms are located in an annex.

*HOTEL PALUMBO*
*Owner: Pasquale Vuilleumier*
*84010 Ravello, Italy*
*tel: (089) 857 244 telex: 770101*
*20 rooms: * Lire 380,000 - 470,000*
*\* Rate includes 2 meals*
*Open: All year*
*Credit cards: all major*
*Delightful villa - superb views*
*Located 66 km S of Naples*

The Villa Cimbrone is not only a hotel: her gardens are one of Ravello's most famous attractions.   The tourist office proclaims, "The Villa Cimbrone, essence of all the enchantment of Ravello, hangs like a swallow's nest on the cliffs."   The villa is reached by a delightful ten-minute walk from the main square of Ravello (the signs are well marked to this favorite sightseeing prize).   Once through the gates, the villa and her magnificent gardens open up like magic.   The gardens are truly superb - if you have ever received postcards from Ravello the chances are they showed the view from the terrace of the Cimbrone.   Most dramatic of all is the belvedere with its stately Roman statues accenting the dazzling view.   Luckily, this outstanding villa is also a small hotel.   The rooms are of museum quality, and even though they do not all have private baths, the furniture is "fit for a king".   The owner, Marco Vuilleumier, gave us a tour of the marvelous old building which is not open to the public - only to the guests.   This fabulous villa was once owned by a British duke and later it was sold to the present owner who told us the following romantic tale: at the end of World War II, the English nobleman landed with the Allied troops in Salerno and as soon as possible found a jeep and wound up the twisting road to see once again his beloved villa.

*VILLA CIMBRONE*
*Owner: Marco Vuilleumier*
*84010 Ravello, Italy*
*tel: (089) 857 138*
*20 rooms: Lire 150,000*
*Open: April through October*
*Fantastic gardens & views*
*Parklike grounds open to the public*
*Located 66 km S of Naples*

The Pensione Villa Maria is perhaps best known for its absolutely delightful terrace restaurant which has a bird's eye view of the magnificent coast. Whereas most of the hotels capture the southern view, the Villa Maria features the equally lovely vista to the north. Although it is a tiny inn, the Pensione Villa Maria is easy to find because it is on the same path which winds its way from the main square to the Villa Cimbrone. After parking your car in the main square of Ravello, look for the signs toward the Villa Cimbrone. If you follow the signs along a path through the village you will find, after about a five minute walk, the Pensione Villa Maria to the right of the path, perched on the cliffs. The building itself is a romantic old villa with a garden stretching to the side where tables and chairs are set - a favorite place to dine while enjoying the superb view. Inside, there is a cozy dining room and upstairs bedrooms which, although simple, all have a private bathroom. The hotel is owned by the gracious Vincenzo and Carla Palumbo who speak excellent English should you call for a reservation. (They also own the more modern, but very pleasant, Hotel Giordano in Positano.) How lucky to be able to have the best of all worlds should you be on a budget - a wonderful view, location, plus a charming villa.

*PENSIONE VILLA MARIA*
*Owners: Carla & Vincenzo Palumbo*
*Sulla Strada per Villa Cimbrone*
*84010 Ravello, Italy*
*tel: (089) 857 170 or 857 255*
*7 rooms: Lire 70,000 - 82,000*
*Wonderful view garden terrace*
*Hilltop town above Amalfi coast*
*Located 66 km S of Naples*

For those of you who love the enchantment of roaming the lakes by boat and getting the first glimpse of your hotel as the boat glides into port, the Hotel Sole is definitely for you.   The Hotel Sole is located on the northern end of Lake Garda in the ancient port of Riva del Garda.   Although the city of Riva has mushroomed to accommodate the influx of tourists, the old section which surrounds the harbor has retained a great deal of medieval charm with colorful old buildings, towers, etc. The hotel is located next to the pier where the ferries dock.   At the rear of the hotel an excellent outdoor terrace looks out over the lake and all its activity.   The hotel is extremely simple, maybe even slightly run-down, but there is a very lovely atmosphere to the hotel and the location is perfect for those who want to stay in the medieval town of Riva and explore Lake Garda by boat.   Its terraces are set with umbrella-canopied tables where one can dine or just enjoy a hot cup of coffee. Who cares if the interior is not a decorator's dream?   You will love sitting all day, watching the show as boats of all shapes, sizes, and colors move in and out of this tiny harbor.

*HOTEL SOLE*
*Owner: Antonio Zampiccoli*
*Manager: Aldo Calderan*
*38066 Riva Del Garda, Italy*
*tel: (0464) 55 26 86*
*25 rooms: Lire 75,000 - 104,000*
*Open: April 11 to October*
*Credit cards: All major*
*Next to the ferry landing*
*N shore of Lake Garda*
*Located 170 km E of Milan*

The Hotel Condotti is located on a tranquil side street near the bottom of the famous Spanish Steps in Rome.   One has the feeling of being in a quiet refuge, away from the hustle and bustle - yet just a block away the neighborhood is a fascinating melange of luxurious shops, restaurants and artists' workshops.   The Hotel Condotti's interior is pretty and fresh, cleverly furnished with a tasteful mixture of old and new.   The lobby features contemporary overstuffed couches topped with colorful pillows, and antique accent pieces such as the inlaid wood reception desk.   A tray with an aperitif selection sits temptingly near the sitting area on a beautiful old escritoire.   This is an intimate city hotel, offering a small number of rooms and personalized service from a staff that is very helpful and speaks very good English.   All the bedrooms are charmingly decorated with white wooden furniture complemented by attractive, vividly colored curtains, bedspreads and upholstery.   A minority of the bedrooms contain bath or shower, thus it is wise to reserve well in advance to receive the desired type of accommodation.   A Continental breakfast is the only meal offered at the Condotti, and it is served in the cheerful breakfast room where bright yellow tablecloths, freshly painted white walls, and original oil paintings create a sunny atmosphere that is a pleasure to wake up to.

*HOTEL CONDOTTI*
*Owner: Ottaviani Hotels*
*Via Mario de'Fiori, 37*
*00187 Rome, Italy*
*tel: (06) 6794661 telex: 611217*
*20 rooms: Lire 146,000*
*Open: All year*
*Credit cards: All major*
*U.S. Rep: Utell International, 800-448-8355*
*Located near the bottom of the Spanish Steps*

If exploring ancient ruins and being able to savor the wonders of Rome's Imperial Forum twenty-four hours a day appeal to you, then the Hotel Forum should be considered for an accommodation in Rome. Although it is not, by official ratings, considered a deluxe hotel (which favorably makes it less expensive than some of Rome's "grand" hotels), it is very attractive. The lobby is especially inviting - more like an exclusive club than a bustling hotel. Dark, wood paneled walls, lush green carpets, beautiful Oriental rugs, a cozy bar, and strategically arranged seating for quiet conversation are all available here. Most of the bedrooms are small and some offer a great view of the old Roman Forum. Perhaps the best feature of all though, is the Forum's wonderful rooftop garden restaurant. Here you can sit in the evening and relax over a leisurely dinner, or, during the day, escape from the bustle of the city by taking a quiet lunch while overlooking the fantastic Roman ruins. (We would appreciate comments from readers concerning the Forum - we have received a letter complaining of very poor service, an extremely small room with worn furnishings and tiny bathroom. In the past, the feedback on this attractive hotel has been very positive so we welcome any comments.)

*HOTEL FORUM*
*Via Tor de'Conti, 25*
*00184 Rome, Italy*
*tel: (6) 6792 446 telex: 622549*
*81 rooms: Lire 224,000*
*Credit cards: All major*
*U.S. Rep: Scott Calder*
*Rep tel: 800-223-5581*
*Perfect location for sightseeing*
*Terrace overlooking Roman Forum*

For location, the Gregoriana is superb: it is situated on Gregoriana Street which runs into the Piazza Trinita dei Monti at the top of the Spanish Steps.   In spite of the perfect location, when I first saw the Gregoriana I just did not see how I could include it in our "inn" book because it has no antique ambiance: in fact, the decor motif might be classified as Chinese with a touch of art deco.   However, after staying at this hotel, I just did not see how I could not include it - it is such a unique little inn and has such a sparkle of personality that it brightens the otherwise somewhat impersonal city of Rome.   You will not be just one of thousands of tourists in Rome - upon arrival, the concierge will probably already know you by name and will continue to greet you personally as you come and go.   Instead of feeling like a face which goes with a key hanging on the wall, you will feel a warmth and intimacy as if you were a guest in a private home.   The rooms are simple but very pleasant and, like the lobby, are decorated with a touch of Oriental ambiance. Those at the rear are especially quiet and some enjoy a balcony with a view over the rooftops of Rome.   Only breakfast is served.   However, there is a concierge on duty twenty-four hours a day to cater to your special needs.

*HOTEL GREGORIANA*
*Owner: Ernesto Panier-Bagat*
*Via Gregoriana, 18*
*00187 Rome, Italy*
*tel: (6) 6794 269 or 6797 988*
*19 rooms: Lire 160,000*
*Breakfast only served*
*Very personalized service*
*Located near top of Spanish Steps*

The Hotel Hassler is a landmark in Rome.  Located in the heart of the elegant shopping area, on the Piazza Trinita dei Monti at the top of the Spanish Steps, this small, elite hotel was once a palatial private home.  Its entrance is sedate and elegant.  The reception rooms are a little somber, but this mood is quickly relieved by a perfectly marvelous inner courtyard - a superb little oasis with stone walls covered with vines, statues, flowers, cozy little tables, and a bar.  You can linger in the garden, take a refreshment in the afternoon or perhaps meet a friend for an aperitif in the evening.  The dining room at the Hassler is also spectacular, boasting one of the finest views in Rome: the entire panorama of the city surrounds you as you dine.  As the evening deepens and the city lights begin to flicker, the scene will become one of romance.  If money is no object, the Hotel Hassler offers some magnificent suites, some with enormous terraces and a view so beautiful that you will be sorely tempted never to set foot from this gorgeous hotel.

*HOTEL HASSLER*
*Manager: Roberto E. Wirth*
*Trinita Dei Monti, 6*
*00187 Rome, Italy*
*tel: (6) 6782 651 telex: 610208*
*100 rooms: Lire 420,000 - 560,000*
*Credit cards: None accepted*
*Beautiful view restaurant*
*U.S. Rep: LHW*
*Rep tel: 800-223-6800*
*Located at top of Spanish Steps*

When we visited the Hotel d'Inghilterra a few years ago, the inside was most appealing although the exterior was quite drab.   On our latest inspection, we were pleased to note that the entrance has been spiffed up and is now much improved. Inside, there is an ambiance of warmth and dignified charm enhanced by strategically placed antiques, lovely paintings decorating the wall, pretty Oriental carpets, antique mirrors and fresh flowers throughout.   Down the hallway is a small bar which seems to be the rendezvous spot for everyone staying at the hotel. This appealing little bar has beautiful dark wood paneling adorned with colorful prints, intimate little tables, fine antique carpets, and comfortable leather sofas. The bedrooms are well decorated in traditional decor.   The location of the d'Inghilterra is excellent.   A short walk in one direction will lead you through lovely shopping avenues to the bottom of the Spanish Steps.   A short walk in the other direction will lead you to the Trevi Fountain with its hubbub of activity. Originally, the Hotel d'Inghilterra was built as a guest house for the famous Torlonia Palace and you will certainly see and appreciate traces of grandeur which are still apparent throughout this once-regal residence.

*HOTEL D'INGHILTERRA*
*Via Bocca di Leone, 14*
*00187 Rome, Italy*
*tel: (06) 672 161 telex: 614552*
*102 rooms: Lire 290,000*
*Credit cards: All major*
*Excellent location - near shopping*
*Located near foot of Spanish Steps*

The Hotel Lord Byron is owned by a fascinating man and superb hotelier, Amedeo Ottaviani, who believes that "Hospitality is like an exquisite flower, it must be surrounded by a thousand delicate attentions" - a concept which transforms each of his hotels into far more than just a place to spend the night.   Each is designed to be a "home away from home" - a quiet sanctuary, well-run and full of character. Ottaviani's chain of small, unique hotels includes the Lord Byron - tucked on a tiny lane surrounded by glamorous homes, it is much more like a private townhouse than a commercial establishment.   The reception desk is discreetly located in the foyer which opens onto an elegant lounge.   An elevator takes guests to the bedrooms, each individually decorated: fabrics, carpets, and the materials used on the custom-built pieces of furniture are carefully chosen to suit the personality and exposure of the room.   Most of the furniture is new - modern yet traditional in feel.   The colors used in fabrics, wall coverings, and carpets are mostly strong, bold colors - frequently with large, bright floral prints, but consistently of excellent quality.   On the lower level is an intimate drawing room-bar where guests can relax before or after dining - adjacent is an elegant restaurant, the Relais Le Jardin, serving without a doubt some of the finest cuisine in Rome.

*HOTEL LORD BYRON*
*Owner: Amedeo Ottaviani*
*Via G. de Notaris, 5*
*00197 Rome, Italy*
*tel: (06) 3609 541  telex: 611217*
*50 rooms: Lire 385,000 - 413,000*
*Open: All year*
*Credit cards: All major*
*U.S. Rep: LHW*
*Rep tel: 800-223-1230*
*Located on edge of Villa Borghese Park*

The very dapper concierge of the Hotel Sistina greeted us in his morning suit of grey striped pants, pearl grey vest, striped tie and black tailcoat.   We found him to be an extremely accommodating fellow, as indeed is the entire staff at the charming Hotel Sistina.   One enters into a tasteful lobby area decorated with greenery in two very large urns, a maroon and gold carpet, and a mix of antique and reproduction furniture.   A very pleasant sitting room adjoins the lobby and guests are invited to relax here at their leisure.   Here comfy couches in colorful floral prints and pretty oil paintings in gilt frames are lit by the soft Venetian glass lamps, and it is a tempting spot to linger.   A new breakfast room was not yet completed at the time of our visit, but it is sure to be as fresh and bright as the rest of the Sistina. In warm weather guests may also enjoy breakfast on the pretty upstairs terrace at umbrella-shaded tables.   Bedrooms, all with modern private baths, are spotless and comfortable although the decor (featuring white walls and contemporary white furniture) is not inspired.   However, some of the rooms are more appealing with very pretty fabrics used for curtains, coverlets and upholstery.   The Hotel Sistina is located on a relatively busy street, and some of the front rooms may suffer from traffic noise; however, the location is very convenient for sightseers and businessmen alike, near the top of the Spanish Steps.

*HOTEL SISTINA*
*Owner: Ottaviani Hotels*
*Via Sistina, 136*
*00187 Roma, Italy*
*tel: (06) 475 8804 telex: 611217*
*27 rooms: Lire 147,000*
*Open: All year*
*Credit cards: All major*
*U.S. Rep: Utell International, 800-448-8355*
*Located near the top of the Spanish Steps*

The gracious Hotel Siviglia enjoys a quiet location three blocks from the central railroad station and across the street from the Russian Embassy in Rome.   In fact, we felt very secure during our stay here, as an armed Italian guard surveys this embassy 24 hours a day.   Built in 1880 as a private residence, the stately, mustard colored facade, pretty lobby and friendly staff provide a warm welcome.   Venetian glass chandeliers, gilt mirrors, and oil paintings dress the lobby and reception areas where armchairs offer a comfortable spot to wait, or simply to recuperate after a day's sightseeing.   Coffees or cocktails can be ordered from the tiny, wood paneled bar area which is part of the main lobby.   On a warm Roman evening, it is a treat to enjoy an aperitif at a table in the adjoining outdoor courtyard filled with flowering plants and statuary.   An elevator or small, sweeping staircase lead to the upstairs rooms, all of which have private bath or shower.   Our room was spacious and lovely with old inlaid wood furniture and a delicate Venetian glass chandelier. Not all the rooms have antiques, but all are tasteful and comfortable with spotless housekeeping evident throughout.   Tall old windows in many of the rooms open onto the central courtyard, while others give views over the rooftops of Rome.

*HOTEL SIVIGLIA*
*Owner: Signora Mongelli Grazia*
*Via Gaeta, 12*
*00185 Rome*
*Italy*
*tel: (06) 4650424 or 4750004 telex: 612225*
*41 rooms: Lire 110,000*
*Open: All year*
*Credit cards: AX VS DC*
*Garden courtyard, bar, elevator*
*Located about 3 blocks N of the railroad station*

San Gimignano is one of the most fascinating of the medieval Tuscany hill towns. Most tourists come just for the day to visit this small town. As you approach, this looks like a city of skyscrapers: come even closer and the "skyscrapers" emerge as 14 soaring towers - dramatic reminders of what San Gimignano must have looked like in all her glory when this wealthy town sported 72 giant towers. If you are lucky enough to be able to spend the night, San Gimignano has a simple but very charming, hotel, La Cisterna. The hotel is located on the main square of town and it fits right into the ancient character of the square with its somber stone walls softened by ivy, arched shuttered doors, and red tiled roof. Inside the medieval feeling continues with lots of stone, vaulted ceilings, leather chairs, and dark woods. The bedrooms are not fancy, but pleasant, and some have balconies with lovely views of the valley. La Cisterna is probably more famous as a restaurant than as a hotel. People come from miles around because not only is the food delicious, but the dining rooms are delightful. Especially charming is the dining room with the brick wall, sloping ceiling supported by giant beams, and picture windows framing the gorgeous Tuscany hills.

*LA CISTERNA*
*Piazza della Cisterna*
*53037 San Gimignano, Italy*
*tel: (577) 940 328*
*46 rooms: Lire 58,000 - 87,000*
*Credit cards: All major*
*Excellent restaurant*
*Hilltown famous for its towers*
*Located 54 km SW of Florence*

The Castel San Gregorio is a sensational, small 12th-century stone castle just a short drive from Assisi, reached after following a winding road through a forest which emerges at the top of a hill to a truly romantic, secluded hideaway.    There is a terrace to the side where tables and chairs are strategically placed to capture a splendid view of the valley far below.    The castle, dating from 1140, has been meticulously reconstructed preserving its original appearance without, and maintaining a castle-like ambiance within.    The hotel is quite dark due both to the character of the building and coverings on many of the walls.    The "old-world" ambiance is further enhanced by the bountiful use of excellent antiques.    The reception desk is in the front lobby: to the left as you enter is an ornate living room; to the right is a dining room where one large table is set each night for the guests to eat together "family style".    A restaurant is located on a lower level, open to the general public, where elegant dining is offered in a beautifully decorated room. The bedrooms I saw, although somewhat dark, were all quite outstandingly decorated with a collection of fine antiques.    Surrounding the hotel are many walking paths leading through the quiet wooded hills.    You will probably not be able to find San Gregorio on any of your maps - the best bet is to find the tiny town of Pianello - San Gregorio is only a few kilometers to the south.

*CASTEL SAN GREGORIO*
*Owner: Bianchi Claudio*
*Via San Gregorio, 16*
*06081 San Gregorio, Italy*
*tel: (075) 803 80 09*
*12 rooms: Lire 81,000*
*Closed: January*
*Credit cards: AX DC*
*Wonderful hilltop castle*
*Located 16 km NW of Assisi*

*Hotel Descriptions*                              179

The Residence San Sano is a small hotel which recently opened in San Sano - a hamlet in the center of the Chianti wine-growing region. Although the finishing touches had not all been completed when we visited, we were charmed by the hotel which is incorporated into a 16th-century stone building. The gracious young owners, Giancarlo Matarazzo and his German wife, Heidi, were both school teachers in Germany prior to returning to Italy to open a small hotel. They have done a beautiful job in the renovation and in the decor. A cozy dining room serves guests excellent meals - featuring typically Tuscan-style cooking. Each of 11 bedrooms is delightfully furnished in antiques and each has a name incorporating some unique feature of the hotel - the name evolving from the time during reconstruction when Heidi and Giancarlo remembered each room by its special feature. My favorite room was the "Bird Room": here birds had claimed the room for many years and had nested in holes which went completely through the wall. With great imagination, the holes were left open to the outside, but on the inside were covered with glass. Now the birds can still nest while guests have the fun of watching the babies. Another room is named for a beautiful, long-hidden Romanesque window which was discovered and incorporated into the decor, another room is named for its very special view, another for an antique urn uncovered - each room displaying great imagination.

*HOTEL RESIDENCE SAN SANO*
*Owners: Heidi & Giancarlo Matarazzo*
*Loc. San Sano*
*53010 Lecchi In Chianti, Italy*
*11 rooms: Lire 100,000 - 115,000*
*Open: All year*
*Credit cards: None accepted*
*Building dates from the 16th century*
*Located 60 km S of Florence*

I know frustratingly little about the Locanda San Vigilio, yet I can hardly wait to return. The day I visited, the owner was away and the man at the front desk insisted that he had strict instructions that no one was to see the hotel. The need for privacy is apparent because its sensational parklike grounds are open to the public and, without protection, the quiet of this small hotel would be invaded by curious tourists. However, my heart was won completely by the charming dining room, elegantly decorated with country antiques and superbly positioned with large windows overlooking the lake. I cannot tell you anything about the 7 bedrooms until I pay another visit to the hotel (hopefully the next time with confirmed reservations). The hotel is part of a gorgeous estate situated on a small peninsula which juts into Lake Garda. You can glimpse the magnificent, private family villa from the path which leads through towering cypress trees to a tiny yacht harbor, next to which is a wonderful, old, two-story building with a red tiled roof and rows of large arched windows capturing views of the lake. I am not sure what the original use this annex served, but now it houses the small hotel, Locanda San Vigilio. I received a letter from the owner which closed with "Our hotel is one of the most beautiful places in Europe, one of the best places for relaxing" - I can certainly believe it.

*LOCANDA SAN VIGILIO*
*Manager: Agostino Guarlenti*
*37016 San Vigilio, Garda, Italy*
*tel: (045) 7255 089  telex: 481874*
*7 rooms: Lire 107,000*
*Open: Easter to October*
*Credit Cards: AX*
*Not suitable for children*
*16th-century lakefront hotel*
*154 km W of Venice, 3 km N of Garda*

The Pitrizza is a tiny jewel of a hotel located on the Emerald Coast of the Island of Sardinia - the playground of the Aga Khan and the jet set of the world. From the moment you enter through the front gate, marked only with a simple little sign, you are in a world of tranquility and beauty. There is a central clubhouse which has a beautiful lounge, a delightful dining room with hand-hewn wooden chairs, a card room, and a bar. A small protected patio extends from the dining room where meals are served when the weather is warm. French doors from the lounge open onto the terrace which leads down to a most unusual swimming pool which is cleverly designed into the natural rock. (The pool is quite wonderful - when in the water the outer edge facing the bay is water level, giving the impression that you are in the sea, not in a pool.) The bedrooms are tucked away in small cottages which blend into the landscape. The rooms are not especially large, but beautiful, with every detail of the finest quality. If your idea of a vacation is a frenzy of activity and "things to do" then the Pitrizza is definitely not for you. There are no planned activities; no sports director; no loud music. Only lovely quiet; gourmet food; a beautiful pool, and a delightful small white sand beach.

*PITRIZZA*
*Manager: Maurizio Maffei*
*07020 Porto Cervo, Sardinia, Italy*
*tel: (0789) 92000 telex: 792079*
*28 rooms: Lire 1,040,000 (rate includes 2 meals)*
*Open: mid-May through September*
*Credit cards: All major*
*U.S. Rep: David B. Mitchell*
*Rep tel: 800-372-1323*
*Pool, beach, tennis available*
*Located on the Island of Sardinia*

Having heard about a lovely little chalet tucked amidst the pines high in the mountains near the French border, I was beginning to wonder what awaited me as the road wound through the ski town of Sauze d'Oulx with its unattractive jumble of modern concrete ski hotels.   However, the road soon left the resort town and continued twisting higher and higher into the mountains until suddenly Il Capricorno came into view nestled in the forest to the left of the road.   Just as you enter there is a tiny bar, and, beyond, a cozy dining room enhanced by dark wooden chalet-style chairs, rustic wooden tables, and a stone fireplace whose wood is stacked neatly by its side.   There is not a hint of elaborate elegance - just a simple cozy country charm.   The perfect kind of inn to come "home" to after a day of skiing or walking the beautiful mountain trails.   The bedrooms, too, are simple but most pleasant with dark pine handmade furniture, neat little bathrooms, and, for a lucky few, balconies with splendid mountain views.   However, the greatest asset of this tiny inn are the owners, Mariarosa and Carlo Sacchi.   Carlo personally made most of the furniture and will frequently join the guests for skiing.   Mariarosa is the chef, and a fabulous, gourmet cook.   This is a very special little hideaway for very special people.

*IL CAPRICORNO*
*Owners: Mariarosa & Carlo Sacchi*
*10050 Sauze d'Oulx, Italy*
*tel: (122) 852 73*
*8 rooms: Lire 107,000*
*Open: Jul to Sep 15 and Dec to May*
*Credit cards: None accepted*
*Tiny inn - very personalized*
*Mountain setting near France*
*Located 218 km W of Milan*

The location of the Grand Hotel dei Castelli is fabulous - high on a hill overlooking not one, but two little bays.   In fact, the hotel dominates the entire peninsula and has a spectacular panoramic walk carved along the cliffs as they circle the parklike grounds.   The views to the crashing surf below are breathtaking.   (If you are with children, hold their hands tightly because there is a perilous drop-off with only a small guard rail for protection.)   In spite of this great location I contemplated not including the hotel because, although it just verges on greatness, it somehow misses - due, I think, to a feeling that the property is not well maintained.   However, the hotel has an absolutely divine outdoor dining terrace which outweighs the lack of perfection in other areas.   On summer nights when the weather is balmy, tables are set out on a balcony which overhangs the side of the cliff and has an incredibly stunning view of the harbor with its yachts and colorful fishing boats.   This terrace is surrounded by trees, so the effect is one of being suspended in air in a tree house with a view of the sea.   The food is marvelous and the service friendly and professional.   As you linger through a delicious meal of fresh fish and watch first the sunset and then the lights across the bay slowly twinkling on, you will probably think the hotel is perfect.

*GRAND HOTEL DEI CASTELLI*
*16039 Sestri Levante, Italy*
*tel: (0185) 410 44*
*45 rooms: Lire 153,000 - 244,000*
*Open: May 15 to October 10*
*Credit cards: All major*
*Natural pool in ocean*
*On the Italian Riviera*
*Located 50 km E of Genoa*

Although the Berghotel Tirol is a new hotel, it happily copies the typical chalet style of the Dolomites. Inside, too, the tasteful decor follows the delightful Alpine motif with light pine furniture, baskets of flowers, and a few antiques for accent pieces. However, what is so very special about the Berghotel Tirol is its marvelous location on a hillside looking over the lovely village of Sexten and to the fabulous mountains beyond. Many of the rooms have large balconies which capture the view and the warmth of the mountain sun. The Berghotel Tirol is not actually in the town of Sexton (sometimes called Sesto on the maps), but in a suburb called Moos. This is one of the most scenic areas of the Dolomites and the town of Sexten one of the most attractive of the mountain towns. In addition to the natural beauty, there is a wonderful network of trails leading in every direction to tempt all into the crisp mountain air. When you return at night to the hotel it is rather like a house party. Most of the guests come for at least a week and table hopping is prevalent as the knicker-clad guests share their day's adventures. Acting as hosts to the "house party" are the extremely gracious, cordial owners, the Holzer family, who seem to be dedicated to seeing that everyone has a good time.

*BERGHOTEL TIROL*
*Owner: Kurt Holzer Family*
*39030 Sexten (Sesto), Italy*
*tel: (0474) 70386*
*30 rooms: * Lire 84,000 to 118,000*
*\* Rate includes 2 meals*
*Open: Dec 20 to Apr 26 and May 20 to Oct*
*Credit cards: None accepted*
*Beautiful mountain valley*
*Dolomites - near Austria*
*2 km SE of Sexton toward Moos*
*Located 44 km E of Cortina*

The Villa Igiea Grand Hotel is an oasis of blissful tranquility in the midst of the large and rather unattractive city of Palermo. With all the fabulous archaeological sites and marvelous cathedrals in the area it is wonderful to have such a splendid hotel to "come home to" at night. The approach to the Villa is not scenic, but from the moment you enter the gates you are in another world: a world of spacious lobbies, sweeping verandas, formal dining rooms, and generously sized, well furnished bedrooms with large modern bathrooms. Many of the bedrooms have private balconies overlooking the gardens to the sea. The hotel is called a villa, but it is much more like a small deluxe castle built right at the edge of the sea. A lovely freeform swimming pool fits itself onto a ledge which overhangs the water. Next to the pool the hotel has its very own ancient Greek temple - now how many hotels can top that? The most outstanding attributes of the hotel are the gardens which envelop the building in a nest of beautiful pines and masses of gorgeous flower beds intertwined with twisting pathways. Altogether, a most delightful hotel.

*VILLA IGIEA GRAND HOTEL*
*Manager: Stefano Baccara*
*Salita Belmonte, 1(Acquasanta)*
*90142 Palermo, Sicily, Italy*
*tel: (091) 543 744 telex: 910092*
*118 rooms: Lire 350,000*
*Credit cards: All major*
*Open: All year*
*Swimming pool, tennis, sea front*
*Own small Greek temple by the sea*
*Located on northern coast of Sicily*

The San Domenico Palace is a super deluxe hotel cleverly incorporated into what was formerly a Dominican monastery. Don't let the monastery bit deter you: absolutely no trace of a life of denial remains. In fact, this is one of the most super deluxe hotels in Italy, catering to your every whim. As you enter the building the lobby opens onto the core of the hotel, the beautiful arcaded Renaissance cloister. Around this inner courtyard the vaulted walkway is now glassed in, but filled with light. Leading off the courtyard are various lounges, writing rooms and game rooms. The dining room is a masterpiece: it has high backed wooden chairs, enormous arched windows and a paneled ceiling. The chapel has been converted into a bar. Throughout the hotel there are priceless antiques of a quality which would make a museum blush with pride. Many of the bedrooms look out to the beautiful bay of Taormina. In the rear of the hotel there is a beautiful garden filled with gorgeous flowers and transected by pathways with small nooks where you can stop to soak in the splendid sea view. A swimming pool is squeezed into the property just as it drops down to the road below. There is no doubt that this is a MOST dramatic hotel.

*SAN DOMENICO PALACE*
*Manager: Romano A. Romani*
*Piazza San Domenico, 5*
*98039 Taormina, Sicily, Italy*
*tel: (0942) 237 01 telex: 980013*
*100 rooms: Lire 378,000*
*Credit cards: All major*
*U.S. Rep: Utell*
*Rep tel: 800-223-9868*
*Swimming pool*
*Located on northern coast of Sicily*

It is hard to be objective when you are "in love" and I fell in love with the Hotel Timeo from the moment I walked through the front gates and into the garden whose bougainvillea trellis covers the pathway to the door.   This is just my kind of hotel, so it is difficult for my personal preferences not to peek through.   The Timeo is a beguiling old villa .   The same family has owned the hotel for over one hundred years and it still maintains the appealing quality of a private home - one loved and cherished by the owners.   The lounges and dining room have many lovely antique pieces.   The bedrooms are not outstanding in decor, but splurge and ask for one with French doors opening onto its own patio.   If you are blessed by sunny days and starlit nights you too will surely fall in love.   The view is incredibly lovely: you look out over the gardens to the shimmering sea far below and, in the distance, proudly dominating the horizon, is Mount Etna.   Note: at the time of publication the Hotel Timeo was closed for renovations.   When we called the hotel, the recording said only that it was being renovated but did not say when the hotel would be open again.   Since it is one of our very favorites, we are keeping it in the book because, hopefully, by the time you are planning a trip it will be open again and be even more beautiful.

*HOTEL TIMEO*
*Manager: Loturco Pancrazio*
*59 Via Teatro Greco*
*98039 Taormina, Sicily, Italy*
*tel: (0942) 238 01   telex: 980073*
*55 rooms: Lire (new rates not published)*
*Credit cards: All major*
*Closed temporarily for renovation*
*Call prior to arrival to check if open*
*Located on eastern coast of Sicily*

The Villa Sant'Andrea is not in the ancient clifftop village of Taormina, but located instead in the village which clusters below. There is a cable car which can whisk you quickly back to Taormina for sightseeing or shopping. (The cable car is only a short block from the hotel so is most convenient.) If you are travelling with children the location is especially nice because the hotel is beautifully positioned at the end of a small swimming cove. In fact the property is built in levels which descend right to the beach where the hotel has its own private section for the guests. You enter the charming old villa from the street level where the reception desk is located. On a lower floor is the dining room which has an informal ambiance with white wicker furniture. The lounge maintains an "English country", look with sofas and chairs upholstered in cheerful floral prints which match the draperies. The bedrooms are simple but many have balconies with beautiful views across the small bay to the dramatic rocks jutting from the brilliant blue water. The hotel was originally built as a private residence for an English family in 1830 and it still maintains the ambiance of an English country estate.

*VILLA SANT'ANDREA*
*Director: Francesco Moschella*
*98030 Taormina, Mazzaro*
*Sicily, Italy*
*tel: (0942) 231 25 telex: 980077*
*36 rooms: Lire 140,000 - 170,000*
*Open: April through October*
*Credit cards: VS AX*
*Own private beach*
*Located on eastern coast of Sicily*

If you would like to combine your sightseeing of Siena with a luxury resort, then the Certosa Di Maggiano might be "just your cup of tea". This is an expensive hotel, but delightful and quite unique. Outside, the hotel looks quite ordinary - just a wall facing the road - but when you step inside it is a fairyland. It doesn't resemble a hotel in the slightest. And it is no wonder: the hotel is built into the restored ruins of a 700-year-old Carthusian monastery. As you enter the arcaded courtyard you can almost see the ghosts of priests, their dark robes flowing, silently walking beneath the vaulted roof of the cloisters. On three sides of the courtyard are arranged the fourteen guest rooms, the lounges, the game rooms, the library, the bar and the exquisite dining room. The fourth side of the courtyard is formed by a small church. The guest rooms are spacious and pleasant but not outstanding in decor. However, the public rooms are smashing, with antiques galore, and all of the finest quality. Another bonus: there is a beautiful pool in the gardens which is never crowded since this is such a tiny hotel. In fact, there are so few people around, that it truly is like being a guest in a private estate.

*CERTOSA DI MAGGIANO*
*Manager: Anna Recordati*
*Via Certosa, 82/86*
*53100 Siena, Italy*
*tel: (577) 288 180 telex: 574221*
*14 rooms: Lire 283,000*
*Closed: November 15 to December 15*
*Credit cards: AX DC VS*
*U.S. Rep: David B. Mitchell*
*Rep tel: 800-372-1323*
*Swimming pool & tennis courts*
*Restaurant only for guests of the hotel*
*Located 68 km S of Florence*

A pensione usually means a compromise in accommodations, so what a delightful surprise the Palazzo Ravizza provides. Even though the government has categorized this hotel as a pensione it is, without a doubt, my choice of where to stay in Siena.  A 17th-century mansion, the Palazzo Ravizza has belonged to the same family for nearly 200 years.  There are only 28 bedrooms, which definitely vary in quality of decor and location.  This is certainly one of the occasions when you will want to request the most deluxe room possible, for, although all rooms are adequate, the ones in the top category are real gems, containing some antique furnishings and possessing lovely panoramic views of the Tuscany hills.  The more expensive rooms are also more tranquil since they overlook the garden rather than the street which can be noisy.  The Palazzo Ravizza is only a short walk from one of the most gorgeous cathedrals in Italy.  It is also only a stroll from the enormous plaza where the running of horses takes place.  The furniture in the small lounge is comfortable and cozy and the dining room is charming.  The total effect is one of excellent taste and marvelous value.  One of the joys of Siena is wandering the intriguing little twisting streets so, although there are several deluxe villa-style hotels in the immediate vicinity, I would stay right in Siena itself since it has such a lovely small hotel.

*PENSIONE PALAZZO RAVIZZA*
*Owner: S. Iannone*
*Plan dei Mantellini, 34*
*53100 Siena, Italy*
*tel: (0577) 280 462*
*28 rooms: Lire 91,000*
*Open: All year*
*Credit cards: None accepted*
*Located in heart of Siena*
*Located 68 km S of Florence*

The Locanda dell'Amorosa makes a wonderful base for exploring the hill towns south of Florence.    It is very accessible since it is located in Sinalunga which is just a few minutes from the expressway between Rome and Florence.    From the Locanda dell'Amorosa it is an easy drive to such sightseeing delights as Siena, Pienza, Orvieto, Todi and Assisi.    However, it is not location alone which makes this hotel so perfect: there is far more.    Truly, the Locanda dell'Amorosa would be marvelous if there were nothing nearby - in fact, the hotel could be a destination in itself.    Actually, this is not a hotel: it is a tiny town a few miles south of Sinalunga. The approach to "town" is a road lined by a majestic row of cypress trees.    Park your car and enter the walls of the 14th-century medieval town where you are greeted by an enormous plaza with its own little church - exquisite inside with its soft pastels and its lovely fresco of the Madonna holding the Christ' child.    To the right of the main entrance to the courtyard are the stables which have been converted to a beautiful restaurant whose massive beams, natural stone and brick walls are original and tastefully enhanced by arched windows, thick wrought iron fixtures and wooden tables.    The guest rooms (located in a separate building to the left of the main entrance) are tastefully appointed with a few antiques and matching bedspreads and draperies.    Most guest rooms have peaceful views of forest and soft green hills.    The rest of this tiny village spreads out behind the main square and the buildings are used for other purposes - including the production of wine.

*LOCANDA DELL'AMOROSA*
*Owner: Carlo Citterio*
*53048 Sinalunga, Italy*
*tel: (0577) 679 497*
*7 rooms: Lire 225,000*
*Closed: January 20 to February 28*
*Credit cards: AX DC VS*
*Located 103 km S of Florence*

As soon as you cross the moat and enter the wonderful medieval village of Sirmione, look to your right. At the end of the street is a sign to the Grifone, a weathered old stone cottage with brown shutters, red-tiled roof, roses creeping up the walls, and a terrace overlooking the lake and castle. Within this quaint building are two separate operations: the simple Hotel Grifone and a small restaurant abounding with antiques and charm. The hotel portion of the house, with an entrance to the rear, has 17 bedrooms on the upper floor. In contrast to the marvelous decor of the restaurant, the hotel is quite drab. The very basic rooms show no warmth or style; however, they each have the luxury of a private bathroom. Also, although this is a budget hotel, it has a prime Sirmione location. What is more, if you are lucky enough to get one of the rooms in the front, you will have the added bonus of a little balcony overlooking one of the finest views in town. Note: we are including this small hotel although we have heard complaints that the hotel never answers letters - this is a problem since, when we call, no one ever seems to speak English. Please let us know your comments.

*HOTEL GRIFONE*
*Owner: Luciano Maracolini*
*25019 Sirmione*
*Lake Garda, Italy*
*tel: (30) 916 014*
*17 rooms: Lire 95,000*
*Open: April 20 to October*
*Credit cards: None accepted*
*Excellent restaurant in building*
*Waterfront location on Lake Garda*
*Located 127 km E of Milan*

What a sense of impending grandeur you experience as you wait for the giant metal gates of the Villa Cortine Palace to swing open.   Once inside the road winds and curves impressively past fountains and statues, flower gardens and mighty trees until you reach the summit where the Villa Cortine Palace reigns.   This beautifully situated villa has been expanded so that the original wing now boasts a new section which appears to have more than doubled the size of the original castle.   Some of the remodeling has a "too modern" feel: one rather wishes that perhaps more of an "old-world" ambiance could have been preserved.   However, in the old section of the villa, which is to the left as you enter the lobby, the rooms still maintain their grandeur with incredibly ornate furniture, soaring ceilings and stunning paintings. Upstairs the guest rooms are large and are decorated with color coordinated drapes, chairs and bedspreads.   What leaves absolutely nothing to be improved upon are the gardens - what a gorgeous sight!   In fact, they are absolutely awe-inspiring.   The villa is surrounded by graveled walkways which wind in and out amongst the fountains, ponds, statues, and glorious rose gardens, all overlooking the lovely lake.

*VILLA CORTINE PALACE HOTEL*
*25019 Sirmione, Italy*
*tel: (30) 916 021 telex: 300171*
*54 rooms: Lire 295,000*
*Minimum stay 3 days*
*Open: April to November*
*Credit cards: All major*
*Swimming pool, tennis, lake pier*
*Park setting - overlooks Lake Garda*
*Located 127 km E of Milan*

The Grand Hotel Excelsior Vittoria has a superb location high on the cliff overlooking the port and bay of Sorrento.   One enters the hotel through a formal gate which is just a short stroll from the center of town.   The hotel is surrounded by an orange grove and park of about four acres with a swimming pool.   The hotel is a grand old villa with a definitely "old-world" atmosphere.   The furnishings, for the most part, continue the antique mood.   Splurge here and get one of the superior rooms with a view of the sea.   The ceilings in some of the reception rooms and in the marvelous airy dining room have gorgeous frescoed designs.   The terraces and gardens surrounding the hotel offer wonderful views, as do the bedrooms which are located facing the bay.   Overall, the hotel has a slightly "worn" look about it but, actually, this fits into the mood of this once magnificent villa. For those of you who want everything perfect, this would not be the hotel for you, but, in my estimation, it is the best in Sorrento.   It will certainly delight anyone who loves the feeling of reliving the grandeur of days gone by in a villa by the sea.

*GRAND HOTEL EXCELSIOR VITTORIA*
*Manager: M. Damiano*
*Piazza Torquato Taso, 34*
*80067 Sorrento, Italy*
*tel: (081) 878 1900 telex: 720368*
*125 rooms: Lire 240,000 - 294,000*
*Open: All year*
*Credit cards: AX VS DC*
*U.S. Rep: Utell International*
*Rep tel: 800-223-9868*
*Beautiful views of Sorrento Bay*
*Swimming pool, elevator to harbor*
*Located 48 km S of Naples*

The road to the Pensione Stefaner winds up a tiny mountain valley in the heart of the Dolomites. The road is gorgeous, but extremely narrow, and twists like a snake around blind curves whose roadside mirrors are a necessity, not an optional precaution. As we rounded the last curve before Tiers the valley opened up and there spread before us a sweeping vista of majestically soaring mountains. Across soft green meadows painted with wildflowers and dotted with tiny farm chalets rose an incredible saw-toothed range of gigantic peaks. Suddenly the journey seemed worth the effort for the scenery alone even if the Pensione Stefaner proved to be a disaster. Luckily, though, the Pensione Stefaner is very nice. The outside is especially attractive - a chalet with flower-laden balconies. Inside, the inn is a bit too "fussy" for my taste, but the valley is so spectacular that I am sure you will be spending most of your time on the beautiful walking trails which lace the valley. The Pensione Stefaner has some antiques scattered throughout for accents, but the furniture is new. The bedrooms are light and airy and many have balconies. Although there was no one who spoke English when I was there, friendliness prevailed. In fact, there was even a gentle, lazy German Shepherd lounging in the lobby offering a friendly welcome.

*PENSIONE STEFANER*
*Owner: Stefaner Family*
*39050 Tiers, Italy*
*tel: (0471) 642 175*
*16 rooms: * Lire 64,000 - 80,000*
*\* Rate includes 2 meals*
*Closed: November*
*New chalet-style inn*
*Lovely mountain setting*
*NE Italy in Dolomites*
*Located 17 km E of Bolzano*

Le Tre Vaselle is a very sophisticated inn located in the small wine town of Torgiano which is very near Assisi. The decor of the hotel is one of a lovely country manor. The owners are the Lungarotti family, famous for their production of superb wines: Mr. Lungarotti owns all of the vineyards around Torgiano for as far as the eye can see. The hotel probably evolved to fill the need for a place for business associates and friends to stay when visiting the vineyards. The accommodations are extremely comfortable and have all the amenities of a large city hotel. The most amazing aspect of Le Tre Vaselle is that it has stunning conference rooms furnished in antiques with intimate adjacent dining rooms. The Lungarotti family has thought of everything: to keep the wives happy while their husbands are in meetings, the hotel schedules cooking classes in one of the most professional kitchens I have ever seen. The Lungarottis also have a private wine museum which would be a masterpiece anywhere in the world. Not only do they have an incredible and comprehensive collection of anything pertaining to wine throughout the ages, but the display is a work of art. The museum alone would be worth a detour to Le Tre Vaselle.

*LE TRE VASELLE*
*Owner: Lungarotti Family*
*06089 Torgiano, Italy*
*tel: (75) 982 447 telex: 660189*
*48 rooms: Lire 235,000*
*Open: All year*
*Credit cards: AX DC VS*
*U.S. Rep: David B. Mitchell*
*Rep tel: 800-372-1323*
*Superb wine museum*
*Located 27 km SW of Assisi, 158 km N of Rome*

The Baia Paraelios is an absolutely delightful hotel tucked onto the spur of land that juts from the toe of Italy near the ancient port of Tropea. The hotel is actually a resort which follows the contours of the hillside from the highway down to the beach. The reception office is located at the top of the hill and the mood is set from the moment you register. The small office is tastefully decorated with plants and charming old prints on the walls and the personnel in the office are gracious and warm in their welcome. The rooms are all bungalows which are artfully terraced down the hill to capture the best view possible from each. Midway down is a lovely pool. At beach level is a beautiful dining room and a comfortable, inviting lounge. The bungalows each have one or more bedrooms, a sitting room and a deck or patio. The decor is simple but in excellent taste with tiled floors and earth tones used throughout. One of the most beautiful white sand beaches I saw in Italy stretches invitingly in front of the complex. The Baia Paraelios makes a nice stop along your route south. Not only will you have the benefit of a lovely break in your travels, but also the nearby ancient town of Tropea, which hangs on the cliffs above a beautiful bay, is fun to explore.

*BAIA PARAELIOS*
*Owner: Adolfo Salabe*
*88035 Parghelia*
*Tropea, Italy*
*tel: (963) 600 004*
*52 bungalows: * Lire  192,000 - 225,000*
*\* Rate includes 2 meals*
*Open: May 10 through September*
*Pool, tennis, gorgeous beach*
*Southern Italy - near tip of toe*
*Located 636 km S of Rome*

In the dramatically beautiful Dolomites of northeastern Italy there are many picturesque villages nestled in the mountains.   Most are filled with attractive, but newly built, houses.   There is one exception.   In the tiny hamlet of Eggen is the Gasserhof Eggen, an old farmhouse (which has been converted into a restaurant) hugging the side of the main road.   Although the building traces its heritage to the 12th century, the interior is plain - a most ordinary looking small restaurant. However, there is a very old, pub-like room whose walls have been blackened from the open fire which extends along one wall which you may see on request.   Rafters overhead, bottle-glass windows, heavy copper pots and rustic wooden country tables and chairs complete the picture of what was at one time the core of the home.   On the outside wall there are remains of very old paintings which at one time probably covered much of the buildings.   Besides the restaurant, there are three rooms sharing one bath, each extremely simple although clean and suitable for travelers on a tight budget.   A nice bonus is the owner's daughter, Inge Weissensteiner, a very pleasant young woman who speaks English.   Note: Eggen is just a few kilometers from Obereggen (see driving instructions under the Hotel Bewallerhof on page 200).

*GASSERHOF EGGEN*
*Owner: Weissensteiner Family*
*39050 Eggen*
*Val d'Ega, Italy*
*tel: (0471) 615 742*
*3 Rooms: Lire 30,000*
*Credit cards: None accepted*
*Restaurant with a few rooms*
*Located 23 km SE of Bolzano*

The Bewallerhof is not a luxury hotel, but an exceptionally appealing small hotel tucked into a remote mountain valley.  The Bewallerhof has it all: a meadow of green velvet stretching out in front to a far vista of beautiful mountains peaks, spectacular giant walls of granite forming the backdrop, wild flowers in the fields, cows munching grass in the distance, birds singing, walking trails spider-webbing out in every direction, pleasant decor, good food, and a large, sunny terrace.  Even with excellent maps, the inn is extremely tricky to find.  Although finding it is half the fun, I will give you a few hints.  The Bewallerhof is located in the Val d'Ega (the Ega Valley) between the towns of Eggen (also called Ega) and Obereggen (also called San Floriano).  If you are driving from Bolzano head southeast through the Val d'Ega for approximately 10 miles watching for the turn to the right for Obereggen.  If you arrive at Nova Levante you have gone too far, so turn back and ask directions.  Should you be coming from Cortina, follow the "Old Dolomite Road" west from Cortina watching carefully for the turnoff toward Nova Levante. When you reach Nova Levante it is only about 3 miles until you reach the road to the left for Obereggen.   These general instructions should help you in pinpointing the town on your own detailed map.

*HOTEL BEWALLERHOF*
*Proprietor: Eisath Family*
*39050 Obereggen (San Floriano)*
*Val d'Ega, Italy*
*tel: (0471) 615 729*
*21 rooms: Lire 98,000 (includes 2 meals)*
*Open: Jul to Oct 15 and Dec 20 to Apr 10*
*Old farmhouse in fabulous setting*
*Surrounded by the Dolomites*
*Located about 25 km SE of Bolzano*

The Gasthof Obereggen, located in the Val d'Ega (Ega Valley) is very simple, but quite wonderful.   The inn is situated on the side of a hill overlooking a gorgeous mountain valley in one of the most beautiful mountain regions of northeastern Italy.   The town of Obereggen is a ski resort and the lift is just a few minutes' walk away.   From the sun-drenched deck which extends generously out from the hotel, there is an absolutely glorious vista across the green meadows to the mountains. Behind the hotel even more majestic mountains poke their jagged peaks into the sky.   Inside there is a cozy dining room.   Mr. Pichler must be a hunter, for trophies line the walls and there is a typical tiled stove against one wall to keep the room toasty on a cold day.   The inn has 12 bedrooms (none with private bath) - those on the second floor open out onto lovely view-balconies.   The greatest asset of this inn, and the real reason for its inclusion, is Mrs. Pichler: she is very special - running her little inn with such a warmth and gaiety that just being in the same room with her is fun.   Mrs. Pichler speaks no English, but her hospitality crosses all language barriers, and her abundant and delicious "home style" cooking speaks to all who love to eat.   Note: Obereggen is almost impossible to find on any map, although the Val d'Ega is usually indicated - please see general driving instructions given under the Hotel Bewallerhof (page 200).

*GASTHOF OBEREGGEN*
*Owner: Pichler Family*
*39050 Obereggen (San Floriano)*
*Val d'Ega, Italy*
*tel: (0471) 615 722*
*12 rooms: Lire 75,000 (includes 2 meals)*
*Credit cards: None accepted*
*Simple inn, wonderful hospitality*
*Beautiful setting in the Dolomites*
*Located 25 km SE of Bolzano*

The Stella d'Italia is located in San Mamete, a tiny, picturesque village nestled along the northern shore of Lake Lugano, just a few minutes' drive from the Swiss border.   The hotel (which has been in the Ortelli family for three generations) makes an excellent choice for a moderately priced lakefront hotel.   Mario Ortelli, an extremely cordial host, showed us throughout the hotel which has two adjoining wings, one quite old and the other a new addition.   My choice for accommodation would be in the original part which has more "old-world" ambiance - the rooms I saw here were very pleasant with large French windows opening onto miniature balconies capturing views of the lake.   The lounges and dining room have a few antique accents, but basically have a modern ambiance.   The nicest feature of the hotel is the superb little lakefront garden - in summer this is where all the guests "live".   Green lawn, fragrant flowers, lacy trees, and a romantic vine-covered trellised dining area make this an ideal spot for whiling away the hours.   Steps lead down to a small pier from which guests can swim.   The ferry dock for picking up and dropping off passengers is adjacent to the hotel.   Another interesting feature for golf enthusiasts is that there are several courses within an easy drive from the hotel - one of these near the town of Grandola is one of the oldest in Italy.

*STELLA D'ITALIA*
*Owner: Mario Ortelli*
*San Mamete*
*22020 Valsoldo*
*Lake Lugano, Italy*
*tel: (0344) 68139 or 61703*
*36 rooms: Lire 77,000*
*Open: April through September*
*Credit cards: All major*
*Lakefront hotel, swimming pier*
*8 km E of Lugano, 100 km N of Milan*

The Pensione Accademia is enchanting - a fairytale villa with delightful gardens, romantic canal-side location, cozy antique-filled interior and professional, caring owners. The hotel has a fabulous setting on an oasis of land almost looped by canals. In front is a beautiful, completely enclosed, "secret" garden whose walls are so heavily draped with vines that it is not until you discover black iron gates that you see steps leading down to the villa's own gondola landing. As you leave the garden and enter the wisteria-covered palazzo, the magic continues with family heirlooms adorning the spacious rooms where sunlight filters through large windows. A staircase leads upstairs where some of the guest rooms are located in the original villa and others, connected by a hallway, in a portion of the hotel borrowed from an adjacent building. No two of the guest rooms are alike, none are "decorator perfect" - they are like guest rooms in a private home. Some of those in the front have canal views but are noisier than those looking over the garden. The only hitch to this picture of perfection is that your chances are slim of snaring a room in this romantic hideaway - the hotel is so special that loyal guests reserve "their" own favorite room for the following year as they leave. Spring and fall are most heavily booked - your chances are better in July and August and the prices are even a little lower.

*PENSIONE ACCADEMIA*
*Manager: Franco Marzollo*
*Dorsoduro 1058*
*3123 Venice, Italy*
*tel: (041) 52 10188*
*26 rooms: Lire 100,000 - 144,000*
*Open: All year*
*Credit cards: All major*
*Beautiful 17th-century palazzo*
*Located near Accademia landing*

The Agli Alboretti Hotel is conveniently located just steps from the Accademia boat landing.   Although only a two star hotel, it has much more charm than many others charging much higher prices.   But it is not price alone that makes the hotel appealing: there is a cozy ambiance from the moment you step into the intimate lobby, paneled with dark mellowed wood and decorated with some attractive prints on the walls and a perky ship model in the window.   At the front desk will be either Dina Linguerri or her daughter Anna.   I did not meet Anna, but her mother is most gracious and speaks excellent English.   Beyond the reception area is a small lounge and then one of the very nicest features of the hotel - a tranquil garden sheltered by an overhanging trellis which in summer is completely covered by vines - a welcome, cool oasis after a day of sightseeing.   In the garden, white wrought iron tables and chairs are set for morning breakfast or afternoon tea.   The guest rooms vary in size, but all have a private bath or shower.   My preference would be one with the small tub, since the shower is the type which does not have a separate enclosure.   Whichever room you have, however, it should be quiet since the hotel is tucked onto a peaceful square.

*AGLI ALBORETTI HOTEL*
*Owners: Dina & Anna Linguerri*
*Accademia 882-884*
*30123 Venice, Italy*
*tel: (041) 523 0058*
*19 rooms: Lire 95,000*
*Closed: 2 weeks in November*
*Credit cards: None accepted*
*Simple hotel with nice courtyard*
*Located near the Accademia boat stop*

The Hotel Do Pozzi has a wonderfully convenient location down a quiet little pathway off the main walkway which leads from St Mark's Square. The hotel has the advantage of being within the heart of Venice and yet in a small world of its own. Taking full advantage of the sun, there is a delightful miniature plaza in a garden setting at the front of the hotel. Inside, the lobby is pleasantly decorated with a small reception desk, Oriental carpets and some comfortable chairs. To the left of the lobby is a lounge area and also a delightful small dining room where guests are served breakfast. The bedrooms are simply decorated in a modern motif - nothing special in their decor - but all with private bath. The bedrooms which face over the little terrace are especially nice. There is no restaurant in the hotel, but this is not a problem since the excellent restaurant, Raffaele's, which is under the same ownership as the hotel, can be reached by a connecting interior entrance: there is no need to venture outside. For someone who wants a moderately priced, beautifully located, pleasant hotel which offers a touch of charm, the Do Pozzi makes an excellent choice.

*HOTEL DO POZZI*
*Owner: Raffaele Restaurant*
*Calle Larga 22 Marzo, 2373*
*30124 Venice, Italy*
*tel: (041) 52 07855 telex: 41027*
*35 rooms: Lire 165,000*
*Credit cards: All major*
*Central location on tiny plaza*

The Hotel Flora is reached down a narrow little alley off one of the main walkways to St Mark's Square, which protects it from the noise of the busy tourist traffic.   At the end of the tiny alley the doors open into a small lobby, beyond which is an enchanting small garden, an oasis of serenity with white wrought iron tables and chairs surrounding a gently tinkling fountain.   Potted plants, small trees and lacy vines complete the scene.   The hotel encloses the garden on two sides: doors open to the right to a dear little bar and the breakfast room.   The lounges are quite Victorian in mood with quite fuzzy dark furniture.   The bedrooms vary in style and size but all are fancy and have quite ornate antique furniture.   Victorian-style wallpaper covers many of the walls, a bit too fancy for my taste, but definitely with an "old-world" feeling.   There is no restaurant at the hotel, which is no problem since Venice abounds with wonderful places to dine.   Breakfast, of course, is served to guests.   The Hotel Flora is a favorite of many travelers to Venice.   I stayed there many years ago and enjoyed it very much - and was pleased to note that it has not changed at all.   Alex Romanelli and his son manage the hotel.

*HOTEL FLORA*
*Owner: Alex Romanelli*
*Calle larga 22 Marzo, 2283/a*
*30124 Venice, Italy*
*44 rooms: Lire 175,000*
*tel: (041) 5205 844  telex: 410401*
*Open: February to November 15*
*Credit Cards: All major*
*No restaurant - breakfast only*
*Delightful inner courtyard garden*
*Located 3-minute walk from St Mark's Sq*

If you love opulent elegance, and if cost is of no consequence to you, then without a doubt the Gritti Palace will be a perfect choice. The location is marvelous too - just a short walk from St Mark's Square yet far enough removed to miss the city's noise and summer mob of tourists. In fact, with careful planning, you can be entirely insulated in a private and very special world from the moment you arrive until you reluctantly depart. If you take a private motor launch from the airport or the Piazza Roma, you can descend stylishly at the deluxe little private pier in front of the hotel where porters will be waiting to whisk you to your room to be pampered and spoiled. All at a price, of course. The Gritti Palace is expensive, very expensive. But then what would you expect when staying in the 15th-century palace of the immensely wealthy Venetian Doge, Andrea Gritti. The Gritti Palace has a charming terrace on the bank of the Grand Canal where you dine in splendor and watch the constant stream of boat traffic. The lobby and lounge areas open off the terrace and are grandly decorated with antiques. The bedrooms too are large and very fancy in decor, and those that face the canal are presented with a 24-hour show.

*HOTEL GRITTI PALACE*
*Campo S. Maria del Giglio, 2467*
*30124 Venice, Italy*
*tel: (041) 52 94611  telex: 410125*
*99 rooms: Lire 485,000 - 680,000*
*Open: All year*
*Credit cards: All major*
*U.S. Rep: CIGA Hotels*
*Rep tel: 800-221-2340*
*Exquisite old palace*
*Canal-front location*
*Located near St Mark's Square*

The Hotel La Fenice et Des Artistes is a real jewel for Venice. Although not inexpensive, it costs much less than many other hotels which do not offer nearly its charm. From the moment you enter the Hotel La Fenice et Des Artistes you will be entranced. The lobby is small, but seems spacious since there are two gay little garden patios which open from it. Here guests sit in the late afternoon for a cup of tea or an aperitif before dinner. The lobby is a triangle which connects the original building with a newer wing. Both sections are very nice, although in summer only the newer wing offers the option of air conditioning, which can be very welcome on a hot day. (There is an additional charge for air conditioned rooms). Off the reception lobby is a nicely decorated lounge and a tiny bar. The bedrooms are not large, but very pleasant and color coordinated with a different wallpaper in each room setting the theme. Breakfast only is served, but this is almost a blessing since within a few blocks there is a wonderful choice of excellent restaurants. The fascinating La Fenice Theater, one of the oldest and most beautiful in Europe, is just around the corner - most conveniently located for music lovers.

*HOTEL LA FENICE ET DES ARTISTES*
*Manager: Dante Appollonio*
*Campiello de la Fenice, S. Marco 1936*
*30124 Venice*
*Italy*
*tel: (041) 52 32333 or 52 26403 telex: 411150*
*75 rooms: Lire 165,000*
*Open: All year*
*Credit cards: None accepted*
*Charming small hotel*
*Located near La Fenice Theatre*

Although La Residenza, with its arched windows, lacy detailing, and columned balcony, is a brilliant example of the finest 15th-century Venetian architecture, I was at first a bit half-hearted in my enthusiasm due to the somewhat dilapidated condition of the small plaza it faces. When I visited the hotel, the massive door was locked and I started to turn away until I discovered a discreetly camouflaged small button incorporated into a brass lion ornament to the left of the door. This I rang and the owner, Franco Tagliapietra, leaned out the window and instructed me in Italian to push open the door when he released the lock. How glad I was that I had persevered. After entering the door and climbing up a flight of stairs, I was magically surrounded by a beautiful, museum-quality room with walls and ceiling adorned with intricate plaster designs. The softly toned walls and the marble floor were enhanced by dark wooden furniture. All of the bedrooms have a private bath and are accented with fine antiques. You might have a problem booking this small hotel, since no one seems to speak English. However, perhaps use the Italian form letter in the back of this guide or get an Italian speaking friend to call for you. This is definitely an excellent value. As a final note, it is no wonder the palace is so splendid - it was the residence of the Gritti family, a most prestigious name in Venice.

*LA RESIDENZA*
*Owner: Franco Tagliapietra*
*Campo Bandiera e Moro*
*30122 Venice, Italy*
*tel: (041) 528 5315*
*15 rooms: Lire 94,000*
*Closed: Nov to Dec 15 and Jan*
*Credit Cards: None accepted*
*Beautiful 15th-century palace*
*A few minutes from St Mark's Square*

The Hotel Panada is tucked down a tiny lane with a most nondescript sign to point the way. However, once you find your way, the hotel is superbly located if you want to be smack in the middle of all the action in Venice - just around the corner from St Mark's Square. In the expensive city of Venice the Hotel Panada stands out as being an excellent value for money. The ambiance surpasses many hotels which charge much higher prices. The outside is quite ordinary, but once inside you will be greeted most hospitably at a small reception desk. To the left of the lobby is an intimate lounge and beyond is a captivating tiny bar with cozy tables set along paneled walls which are enhanced by the romantic reflections of flickering lights in an array of small framed mirrors. This small bar provides a delightful respite to rest the feet and have a cool drink after a day of sightseeing. But it is not only the downstairs that is pleasant: the bedrooms are all similarly decorated with cream colored walls which attractively set off Venetian-style handpainted beds, chests and desks. As a final touch, venetian-glass chandeliers light the rooms. A final note: there is no restaurant at the hotel although light snacks can be ordered at the bar. The hotel is, however, surrounded by inviting restaurants.

*HOTEL PANADA*
*Proprietor: A Caputo*
*Calle Specchieri, 463*
*San Marco 646*
*30124 Venice, Italy*
*tel: (041) 52 09088  telex: 410153-Panada*
*45 rooms: Lire 173,000*
*Open: February through December*
*Credit Cards: All major*
*1 block from NE corner of St Mark's Square*

At first glance the Pensione Seguso appears quite simple: a rather boxy affair without much of the elaborate architectural enhancements so frequently evident in Venice. However, the inside of the pensione radiates warmth and charm and elegant taste. The hotel is located on the "left bank" of Venice - across the Grand Canal from the heart of the tourist area, about a 15-minute walk to St Mark's Square (or only a few minutes by ferry from the Accademia boat stop). For several generations the hotel has been in the Seguso family who do a marvelous job in providing a homelike ambiance for the guest who does not demand luxury, but appreciates quality. One delightful surprise is that this hotel has so much to offer. In front there is a miniature terrace harboring a few tables set under umbrellas. Several of the bedrooms have wonderful views of the canal (although these rooms are the noisiest due to the canal traffic). The most pleasant surprise is that the value-conscious tourist can stay at the Pensione Seguso with breakfast and dinner included for what the price of a room alone would cost for most hotels in Venice. I recently revisted the Pensione Seguso and was delighted to find it even prettier than I had remembered. Although mellowed with age, this hotel gleams with the refinement of a beautiful family home, with Oriental rugs setting off dark wooden antique furniture and excellent heirloom silver services.

*PENSIONE SEGUSO*
*Owner: Seguso Family*
*Grand Canal Zattere, 779*
*30123 Venice, Italy*
*tel: (041) 52 22 340 or 52 86 858*
*36 rooms: * Lire 134,000 - 151,500*
*\* Rate includes 2 meals*
*Credit cards: None accepted*
*Easy walk from the Accademia boat stop*

The Casa Frollo, located on Giudecca Island across from St Mark's Square, is a real gem: a moderately-priced oasis just minutes from the heart of Venice. Once you arrive at Giudecca Island (getting off at the Riva degli Schiavoni dock), walk to your right and you will see the Casa Frollo. You enter through huge doors and then climb the stairs to your right to bring you into an enormous reception - all-purpose room. The owner, Flora Soldan, is frequently at the desk as you enter. She can understand a little English, but if you have a problem communicating, her son Pablo who understands better is usually close at hand. My heart was won the moment I stepped into the room which is brimming with priceless antiques and was enveloped by its awesome size. The room runs the length of the building and the front windows (where tables are set for breakfast and drinks) open onto a sensational view of Venice. The rear windows open onto a lazy, lush garden. For those on a tight budget, there are some rooms without baths. For budget splurgers, request a bath and a view of Venice.

*CASA FROLLO*
*Manager: Marino Soldan*
*Fondamenta Zitelle, 50*
*Giudecca, 50*
*30123 Venice, Italy*
*tel: (041) 2 22723*
*26 rooms: Lire 75,000 - 92,000*
*Open: March 18 to November 21*
*Credit cards: None accepted*
*17th-century palace*
*Splendid view of St Mark's Square*
*Located on Giudecca Island*

The Hotel Cipriani was founded by the late Giuseppe Cipriani, who during his lifetime became almost a legend in Venice.   This beloved man, who founded the internationally famous Harry's Bar in Venice, had a dream of building a fabulous hotel within easy reach of St Mark's Square and yet far enough away to guarantee seclusion and peace.   He bought three acres on the island of Giudecca and with the financial assistance of some of his prestigious friends, such as Princess Brigit of Prussia and the Earl of Iveagh (head of the Guinness brewing company in Dublin), he accomplished his dream - an elegant Venetian palace-style hotel. The Cipriani is the perfect hotel for those of you who MUST have a pool, for it is the only hotel with a pool in Venice.   And what a pool - it is Olympic size and surrounded by beautiful gardens.   The splendor continues inside where the lounges are tastefully decorated in whites and beiges and the bedrooms are large and elegant.   You truly have the best of all worlds at the Cipriani - you are at a superior resort yet only minutes from the heart of Venice in the private launch which waits to whisk you, any time of the day or night, to St Mark's Square.

*HOTEL CIPRIANI*
*Manager: Dr. Natale Rusconi*
*Isola della Giudecca, 10*
*30123 Venice, Italy*
*tel: (041) 52 07 744  telex: 410162*
*98 rooms: Lire 470,000 - 710,000*
*Open: February 27 to November 10*
*Credit cards: AX*
*U.S. Representative: LHW*
*Rep tel: 800-223-6800*
*Swimming pool, lovely gardens*
*Located on Giudecca Island*

If the idea of being close to Venice and yet near a beach and casino appeals to you, then perhaps you should consider a hotel located on the Lido, a small island opposite St Mark's Square. A fifteen-minute boat ride and a short taxi trip brings you to the Albergo Quattro Fontane, a charming inn which reminds me more of a French country home than an Italian villa. It has a white stuccoed exterior with gabled roof, green shutters, and vines creeping both over the door and around some of the small balconies. To the left of the main building is a lovely courtyard whose privacy is established by another wing of the hotel giving the garden a cozy, "walled in" effect. Inside the hotel there is an ambiance of a country home with antiques cleverly used throughout the lounges. The beach is only a short distance away and the Albergo Quattro Fontane can make arrangements for you to reserve a private beach cabana when you arrive at the inn. The cost per day will vary, depending both upon the location and the comparative luxury of the cabana you choose. The beach is wide and the water clear, although the sand is not as fine and white as many of our American beaches. Still, it is quite an experience just to sample the interesting hierarchy of the Italian beach system.

*ALBERGO QUATTRO FONTANE*
*Via 4 Fontane*
*30126 Lido of Venice*
*Venice, Italy*
*tel: (041) 52 60227 telex: 411 006*
*70 rooms: Lire 190,000 - 250,000*
*Open: end of April to October 1*
*Recently all the rooms have been air conditioned*
*Near casino, beach, tennis*
*Located on the Lido, across from Venice*

The tiny island of Torcello is located about fifty minutes from Venice by boat. This lovely, sleepy little island is usually considered a short stop for the tour boats as they ply their way among the maze of little islands surrounding Venice.    But, for those who want to linger on Torcello, where they can be close to Venice yet feel out in the country, there is a deluxe inn which is owned by the Cipriani family.    This small inn, the Locanda Cipriani, is well known to knowledgeable gourmets as a fantastic restaurant.    Many arrive every day from Venice just to dine, and depart never knowing that upstairs this restaurant also has guest rooms.    The inn is very simple, much more like a small farmhouse than a deluxe hotel.    Inside there is a rustic, cozy dining room and outside a beautiful dining terrace surrounded by gardens brilliant in summer with all varieties of flowers.    There are only a few bedrooms which are all suites.    Breakfast and dinner are included in the room rate.    This is an expensive inn, but an elegant hideaway for relaxing and dining royally in a beautiful country setting.    Many famous guests have already discovered this oasis - including Hemingway, who came here to write.    I think you will share his belief that the Locanda Cipriani Torcello is a very special place.

*LOCANDA CIPRIANI TORCELLO*
*Owner: Cipriani Family*
*Manager: Bonifacio Brass (son)*
*30012 Isola Torcello*
*Venice, Italy*
*tel: (041) 52 30150*
*5 suites: Lire 460,000 (includes 2 meals)*
*Open: mid-March to mid-November*
*Credit cards: VS*
*Luxury inn on quiet little island*
*Reached by boat from Venice*

The Hotel due Torri is not a cozy little inn, but it is unique and has its own style. You enter into an enormous central inner court which is almost like a football field - a football field with a floor of large rust and cream colored tile that looks like a chessboard. Encircling the room are columns supporting arches which form an arcade. The ceiling is covered with brilliant paintings. Bright green and red comfortable lounge chairs form small groupings for conversation. After the initial impact, the room begins to "grow on you", especially when you read the history and realize that in the 14th century the Lords of Verona used this building as their official guest house. The bedrooms are even more unusual than the lobby. Each has genuine antique furniture meticulously collected to maintain authenticity. Each of the bedrooms has a different decor: most feature very ornate furnishings. Some of the rooms are Louis XVI style, others Greek-Roman, others Charles X period, others English. But all have real antiques. To make this choice of rooms even more fun, there is a set of slides in the lobby where you can look at the pictures of the various rooms and pick out one that especially suits your mood. (If the hotel is not filled, of course.)

*HOTEL DUE TORRI*
*Owner: Enrico Wallner*
*Manager: R. Giavarini*
*Piazza San Anastasia*
*37100 Verona, Italy*
*tel: (45) 595 044  telex: 480524*
*100 rooms: Lire 338,000*
*Open: All year*
*Credit cards: All major*
*Authentic antiques used throughout*
*Located in the heart of Verona*

The entrance to the Hotel Victoria is starkly modern - almost with a museum-like quality.    The white walls, white ceiling, white floors, and an enormous skylight are softened by the green plants.    At first glance I was disappointed since I had heard so many glowing reports of the merits of this small hotel.    However, the mood begins to change as you enter the reception area with its Oriental carpets and, by the time you arrive in the lounge area, the feeling is definitely moving toward an antique ambiance with the original heavy ancient wooden beams and one of the original stone walls exposed, leather chairs, and some lovely antique tables.    The bedrooms are extremely modern and beautifully functional with good reading lights, comfortable chairs, and excellent bathrooms.    The Victoria actually dates back centuries and the new hotel is built within the shell of an ancient building. The architect even incorporated some of the archaeologically interesting finds of the site into a museum in the basement level.    When the hotel is not full and all of the dining room tables are not needed, special "windows" open up on the floor of the restaurant and the museum below is lit so that you can study the artifacts as you dine.

*HOTEL VICTORIA*
*Manager: Rodolfo Zema*
*Via Adua, 8*
*37121 Verona, Italy*
*tel: (45) 590 566  telex: 431109*
*44 rooms*: *Lire 170,000*
*Open: All year*
*Credit cards: AX DC*
*U.S. Rep: Jane Condon*
*Rep tel: 800-223-5608*
*Located in heart of Verona*

The Hotel Turm belongs to the Romantik Hotel Chain.   Just being a member of this exclusive "club" indicates the hotel is pretty special because to belong the inn must have the owner personally involved in the management and the interior must have an antique ambiance.   The Hotel Turm is no exception.   There is an especially attractive little dining room with vaulted whitewashed ceilings and chalet-style rustic wooden furniture.   There are a few antiques in the hallways and lounges.   The bedrooms are simple, but very pleasant, with light pine furniture and fluffy down comforters on the beds.   There is a swimming pool on the terrace where one can swim or lounge while gazing out to the little town and the mountains beyond.   There is even a small indoor pool.   The Hotel Turm dates back to the 13th century and Mr. Pramstrahler takes great care to maintain touches of the "old-world" charm by interspersing antique chests, cradles, chairs and ancient artifacts.

*ROMANTIK HOTEL TURM*
*Owner: Pramstrahler Family*
*1-39050 Vols am Schlern*
*Sudtirol, Italy*
*tel: (0471) 72 014*
*24 rooms: Lire 86,000 - 123,000*
*Closed: November to end of December*
*Credit cards: VS*
*U.S. Rep: Romantik Hotel*
*Rep tel: 800-826-0015*
*Indoor and outdoor pools*
*Mountain setting NE of Bolzano*

# Inn Discoveries from Our Readers

Although this new edition of *Italian Country Inns & Villas* reflects the results of two recent research trips to Italy, we still have a few last-minute hotels we want to share with you. Many of the hotels newly featured in this edition are those you recommended to us and which we inspected and agreed wholeheartedly with your appraisal. However, there were some we never had the opportunity to see (sometimes your letters arrived after we had returned from Italy and sometimes we did not have enough time to travel to the specified location). We have a rule never to include any hotel, no matter how perfect it sounds, until we have made a personal inspection. This seemed a waste of some excellent "tips", so, to solve this dilemma, we have added to each of our guides a new section of hotels you have discovered and have shared with us but which we have not yet had the opportunity to visit. Thank you for your contributions. Please keep them coming.

## ACQUAFREDDA          HOTEL VILLA CHETA ELITE

Hotel Villa Cheta Elite, Strada Statale, Acquafredda, 85041 Potenza, Italy, tel: (0973) 878 134, Open April - September, 20 rooms: Lire 85,000.

We had targeted the Hotel Villa Cheta Elite as a potential "to see" for this edition, but our research did not take us to the south of Italy. Since we were disappointed not to have had time to visit this hotel (located in one of our favorite coastal areas in southwestern Italy), it was a welcome surprise to receive a call from a reader who had stayed at the Villa Cheta Elite. Being from the "Old Country" herself, she said, "From an Italian's point of view, the hotel is absolutely delightful. The handsome owners are warm and gracious, and, although they speak no English, are excellent hosts to all the guests." We can hardly wait to try out the hotel ourselves, and in the meantime we will appreciate remarks from other readers.

## ASOLO HOTEL DUSE

Hotel Duse, 31011 Asolo, Treviso, Italy, tel: (0423) 55241, 13 rooms: Lire 87,000.

While I was on the ferry between Giudecca Island and Venice, guests from the Casa Frollo were sharing the ride. Eager to hear how they liked the hotel which I had just visited, we began to talk about places to stay. Yes, they very much liked the Casa Frollo, but they also told me about another inn, one of their favorites, located a little north of Venice in the romantic medieval village of Asolo. Since Asolo is such a delightful town, it was nice to hear that in addition to the Villa Cipriani (which is already in our guide), there is another hotel, the Duse, which they thought absolutely delightful. The Hotel Duse is a less expensive hotel, so it is nice to be able to add an alternate possibility for Asolo. I will be eager to go myself to check it out....soon, I hope.

## BARBERINO VAL D'ELSA FATTORIA "CASA SOLA"

Fattoria "Casa Sola", 50021 Barberino Val d'Elsa, Italy, tel: (055) 8075 028, Owners: Jeffe and Claudia Gambaro, Open May - October.

On our last trip to Italy we fell in love again with Tuscany - the enticing wine-growing region south of Florence. It was frustrating to leave because each day we would hear of another enchanting place to investigate. Our next book will delve in depth into staying in these romantic Tuscany farmhouses which have opened their doors to "paying guests", but in the meantime it is fun to mention a farm with rooms recommended by a reader. "We particularly liked the Casa Sola which is located near the village of San Donato in Poggia, halfway between Florence and Siena. The house is part farmhouse (probably built in the 18th century) and part more formal villa, presumably from the 19th or 20th century. There are three or four bedrooms (perhaps more), a bathroom, large living room (rather sparsely furnished), a dining room and kitchen. The furnishings are slightly shabby, but pleasant. We had the place completely to ourselves except that the owners came for one night and the farmer and his wife lived in the older part of the house. We made our own beds and got our own meals (and drank Casa Sola Chianti). The countryside is beautiful and on a clear day you can see the towers of San Gimignano in the distance from the windows. I imagine that they want to rent the place for at least a week at a time. A nearby restaurant we liked very much was the Trattoria La Toppa in San Donato (tel: (055) 807 2900). This ancient trattoria offers genuine home cooking prepared with first quality ingredients according to recipes that the cook-owners, Carla and Mariarosa, have learnt from their mothers and grandmothers." *Recommended by David Yerkes.*

## MALEO          ALBERGO DEL SOLE

Albergo del Sole, 20076 Maleo, Milan, Italy, tel: (0377) 581 42, Owners: Franco and Silvana Colombani, 8 suites: Lire 180,000.

Just a few days before this latest edition of *Italian Country Inns & Villas* went to press, we received a delightfully written long letter from Ann Berman, a friend of Franco and Melly Solari (whose outstanding "restaurant with rooms" is newly featured in this guide - see page 118). Ann and her husband have travelled extensively in northern Italy and have developed close relationships with the owners of several of the top restaurants in the countryside and in the small cities. She mentioned several favorites including the Albergo del Sole, located about an hour's drive south of Milan, about which she wrote the following: "Franco and Silvana Colombani of the Albergo del Sole in Maleo have long been respected for having one of the finest restaurants in Italy: Franco is recognized as the father of the move to regional cuisine (which he never deserted) and the founder of the

Linea Italia in Cucina. He has a Michelin star and the praise of the Italian guides and journalists for many years. He has recently renovated the restaurant, uncovering much of the original physical structure dating back to the 15th century. In addition, he has built eight suites for patrons (four are completed and the remaining four will be completed in the next several months). Over the past ten years we have stayed there numerous times (and eaten perhaps 100 meals there), stays ranging from overnight to two-week visits. The rooms are wonderfully comfortable and decorated simply and elegantly with all the comforts that a luxurious country inn should provide. Franco is a warm and friendly host, and the staff is professional and helpful. The location is perfect for visits to Cremona , one of the under-appreciated cities of northern Italy; it is also a perfect stopover on the way to or from the Milan airport if one is visiting Tuscany or other points in northern or central Italy. It is also, of course, wonderful just to stop there to eat and to drink, knowing that a comfortable room awaits you after your meal." *Recommended by Ann E. Berman.*


## MONTELUCO DI SPOLETO        HOTEL PARADISO

Hotel Paradiso, 06049 Monteluco di Spoleto, Italy, tel: (0743) 371 82, Owner: Mario Giammari, 24 rooms: Lire 60,000.

"The Hotel Paradiso is located in the town of Monteluco, which is directly across the autostrada from Spoleto. The hotel is in a lovely wooded area. There's direct bus service into Spoleto. We had a nice breakfast, although we did not try other meals which are available. The quiet atmosphere was particularly nice when Spoleto was so noisy and jammed with tourists during the festival." We received some pictures of the Hotel Paradiso which appears to be a handsome stately mansion set in a forested area. *Recommended by Diana Clark.*

Hotel Laudomia, Poderi di Montemerano, 58050 Grosseto, Italy, tel: (0564) 620 062, 12 rooms: Lire 55,000.

We received a wonderful letter from Texas from a reader who shared with us a "restaurant with rooms" that sounds most interesting - especially for those who love a good restaurant and are not too fussy about the rooms. "The Concierge at the Hotel Bristol in Sorrento sent us to the tiny Italian village of Poderi di Montemerano when I asked for a recommendation of someplace tourists didn't go. The place is called Hotel Laudomia, and is simply a few rooms (quite plain but with some antique furnishings) added in an old building across the road from a small restaurant (of the same name) that became so popular with natives from various parts of Italy who came to eat, that a few guest rooms were added. The restaurant was phenomenal - the building it is in and the main dining room both look like something out of a storybook. Absolutely *NO ONE* in the place spoke English - we spoke no Italian, but had a wonderful time. The food was superlative. In the room there was a fireplace, fresh flowers in an old copper pot sitting in the window, and framed art all over the walls. The town of Poderi di Montemerano is miniscule, just a few lanes to walk up. It is only about two hours from Rome and not far from the eastern coast." One of the reasons Hotel Laudomia interests us so much, is that on one of our research trips we tried diligently, without success, to find a hotel in this area of Italy which is quite off the beaten track of most Americans. *Recommended by Sally Watkins*.

## ROME          LA RESIDENZA

La Residenza, Via Emilia, 22-24, 00187 Rome, Italy, tel: (06) 679 9582, 27 rooms: Lire 145,000.

We had seen La Residenza a few years ago when the first edition of our Italian guide came out.   At that time, the hotel was full and we were not able to see any of the guest rooms nor was the manager available to chat with us - so we weren't able to get a "feel" for the hotel and did not include it.   However, we have received several recommendations from readers, including Therese Reynolds, who says "La Residenza is charming and a super buy.   It is really more like a private club than a hotel and many of the rooms even have their own terrace or patio.   The location is good too - near the Via Veneto and the American Embassy."   The brochure enclosed with Therese's note refreshed our memories of a small hotel with a cozy "homelike" ambiance   *Recommended by Therese Reynolds.*

## SIENA          HOTEL SANTA CATERINA

Hotel Santa Caterina, Via Enea Silvio Piccolomini, 7, 53100 Siena, Italy, tel: (0577) 22 11 05, 19 rooms: Lire 149,000 - 169,000.

For those of you who like to be within walking distance of all the fascinating sights that Siena has to offer, we are glad to be able to mention another hotel choice. Already included in our guide is the Pensione Palazzo Ravizza whose owners have recently opened another hotel, the Santa Caterina, which had been recommended by several readers.   This new hotel, which was originally an 18th-century villa, is located just outside one of the main entrances into Siena, the Porta Romana. *Recommended by S. Iannone.*

Imperial Tramontano Hotel, via Vittorio Veneto, 80067 Sorrento, Italy, tel: (081) 878 1940, 109 rooms, Open April through October.

The Grand Hotel Excelsior Vittoria (referred to in this letter) is already in our guide, but space is not always available - especially during the tourist season. Therefore, we are especially glad to have the following recommendation:  "On your next visit to Italy, you may want to check out the Imperial Tramontano Hotel in Sorrento.   I cannot believe that the Grand Hotel Excelsior Vittoria is any better. We had a room that had a sitting room, bedroom and huge bathroom with two balconies, one in the sitting room and one in the bedroom, overlooking the harbor, Capri and Vesuvius all for $107.00 per night (October 1987).   The facilities are wonderful, the lobby is beautiful and there is greenery surrounding the entrance to the establishment." *Recommended by Debby Lumkes.*

Residenza di San Andrea al Farinaio, Terontola di Cortona, Italy, tel: (0575) 677 736, Owner: Patrizia Nappi, 5 bedrooms:   Lire 65,000, No credit cards, Open all year.

Our final recommendation comes from a reader in Canada who enclosed with her wonderful long letter a brochure of the Residenza di San Andrea al Farinaio, such an appealing small inn that I wanted to return immediately to Italy to see it for myself.   The description goes as follows: "The Residenza di San Andrea al Farinaio is a 12th-century manor that was built on a rather historic location - on the grounds of an earlier church, San Andrea, and a couple of kilometers from where Hannibal on his elephant is said to have led his army against the Romans.   Many of the paintings of the church now hang in the manor.   One of the most striking and appealing features is the harmonious and thoughtful way in which the art and artifacts of the old world have been placed together with the new. The owner, Patrizia Nappi, is a gracious, elegant woman whose care and good tase in her own life extend to the ambiance of her home. Her hospitality is unequalled. In the short time that we stayed (five days), she became more an acquaintance than an innkeeper. She is very fond of dogs, and owns about seven, most of whom are alternately placed in a confined area. (So, a word of warning to those allergic to dogs.) The grounds cover an impressive four hectares, where she grows an array of fruit, including grapes, pomegranates, and figs. She has hired people to help her maintain her property, including making her own wine, which is a high-quality Denominazione dei Origine Controllata (Valdichiana). The house holds only five double bedrooms for guests. Although we had a private bath, I don't know how many other rooms had one. The place is fully renovated, retaining much of the antique features of the manor, like the beamed ceiling and the hard-tiled floors. Because of the size of the inn, it would be wise to write to Patrizia Nappi ahead of time to book. She has a number of American guests that return almost every year, and stay for weeks. I don't wonder." *Recommended by Angie McElwain.*

# HOTEL RESERVATION REQUEST LETTER IN ITALIAN

**HOTEL NAME & ADDRESS** - clearly printed or typed

*Vi prego di voler riservare:*       I would like to request:

_____
*Numero delle camere con bagno o doccia privata*
Number of rooms with private bath/shower

_____
*Numero delle camere senza bagno o doccia*
Number of rooms without private bath/shower

_____
*Numero delle persone nel nostro gruppo*
Number of persons in our party

_____ *Data di arrivo*    _____ *Data di partenza*
Arrival date                 Departure date

*Vi prego inoltre de fornirmi le seguenti informazioni:*
Please let me know as soon as possible the following:

| | | |
|---|---|---|
| *Potete riservare le camere richieste?* | *SI* | *NO* |
| Can your reserve the space requested? | yes | no |

*Prezzo giornaliero*
Rate per night _____

| | | |
|---|---|---|
| *I pasti sono compresi nel prezzo?* | *SI* | *NO* |
| Are meals included in your rate? | yes | no |
| *E necessario un deposito?* | *SI* | *NO* |
| Do you need a deposit? | yes | no |

*Quanto e necessario come deposito?*
How much deposit do you need _____

*Ringraziando anticipatamente, porgo distinti saluti,*
Thanking you in advance, I send my best regards,

**YOUR NAME & ADDRESS** - clearly printed or typed

# Index - Alphabetically by Hotel

*Index Alphabetically by Hotel*

*Index Alphabetically by Hotel*

# Index - Alphabetically by Town

*Index Alphabetically by Town*   233

*Index Alphabetically by Town*

*Index Alphabetically by Town*

# INN DISCOVERIES FROM OUR READERS

Future editions of *KAREN BROWN'S COUNTRY INN GUIDES TO EUROPE* are going to include a new feature - a list of hotels recommended by our readers. We have received many letters describing wonderful inns you have discovered; however, we have never included them until we had the opportunity to make a personal inspection. This seemed a waste of some marvelous "tips". Therefore, in order to feature them we have decided to add a new section called "Inn Discoveries from Our Readers".

If you have a favorite discovery you would be willing to share with other travellers who love to travel the "inn way", please let us hear from you and include the following information:

1. *Your name, address and telephone number.*

2. *Name, address and telephone number of "your inn".*

3. *Brochure or picture of inn (we cannot return material).*

4. *Written permission to use an edited version of your description.*

5. *Would you want your name, city and state included in the book?*

In addition to our current guide books, we are also researching future books in Europe and updating those previously published. We would appreciate comments on any of your favorites. The types of inns we would love to hear about are those with special "olde-worlde" ambiance, charm and atmosphere. We need a brochure or picture so that we can select those which most closely follow the mood of our guides. We look forward to hearing from you. Thank you.

# Karen Brown's Country Inn Guides to Europe

## The Most Reliable & Informative Series on European Country Inns

Detailed itineraries guide you through the countryside and suggest a cozy inn for each night's stay. In the hotel section, every listing has been inspected and chosen for its romantic ambiance. Charming accommodations reflect every price range, from budget hideaways to deluxe palaces.

# *Order Form*

## KAREN BROWN'S COUNTRY INN GUIDES TO EUROPE

Please ask in your local bookstore for **KAREN BROWN'S COUNTRY INN** guides.
If the books you want are unavailable, you may order directly from the publisher.

*AUSTRIAN COUNTRY INNS & CASTLES  $12.95*
*ENGLISH, WELSH & SCOTTISH COUNTRY INNS  $12.95*
*EUROPEAN COUNTRY CUISINE - ROMANTIC INNS & RECIPES  $12.95*
*EUROPEAN COUNTRY INNS - BEST ON A BUDGET  $14.95*
*FRENCH COUNTRY INNS & CHATEAUX  $12.95*
*GERMAN COUNTRY INNS & CASTLES  $12.95*
*IRISH COUNTRY INNS  $12.95*
*ITALIAN COUNTRY INNS & VILLAS  $12.95*
*PORTUGUESE COUNTRY INNS & POUSADAS  $12.95*
*SCANDINAVIAN COUNTRY INNS & MANORS  $12.95*
*SPANISH COUNTRY INNS & PARADORS  $12.95*
*SWISS COUNTRY INNS & CHALETS  $12.95*

*Name* _____    *Street* _____

*City* _____    *State* _____  *Zip* _____

*Add $2.00 per copy for postage & handling.  California residents add sales tax.*
*Indicate the number of copies of each title.  Send in form with your check to:*

TRAVEL PRESS
P.O Box 70
San Mateo, CA  94401
(415) 342-9117

*This guide is especially written for the individual traveller who wants to plan his own vacation. However, should you prefer to join a group, Town and Country - Hillsdale Travel can recommend tours using country inns with romantic ambiance for many of the nights' accommodation. Or, should you want to organize your own group (art class, gourmet society, bridge club, church group, etc.) and travel with friends, custom tours can be arranged using small hotels with special charm and appeal. For further information please call:*

*Town & Country - Hillsdale Travel*
*16 East Third Avenue*
*San Mateo, California 94401*

*(415) 342-5591*
*Outside California 800-227-6733*

**KAREN BROWN** travelled to France when she was 19 to write *French Country Inns & Chateaux* - the first book of what has grown to be an extremely successful series on European country inns. With 12 guides now on the market, Karen's staff has expanded, but she is still involved in planning, researching, formatting and editing each of the guides in her Country Inn series and returns frequently to Europe to update her guides. Karen, her husband, Rick, and their daughter, Alexandra, live in the San Francisco Bay area.

**CLARE BROWN**, CTC, has many years of experience in the field of travel and has earned the designation of Certified Travel Consultant. Since 1969 she has specialized in planning itineraries to Europe using charming small hotels in the countryside for her clients. The focus of her job remains unchanged, but now her expertise is available to a larger audience - the readers of her daughter's Country Inn guides. Clare lives in the San Francisco Bay area with her husband, Bill.

**BARBARA TAPP** is the talented artist responsible for the interior sketches of *Swiss Country Inns & Chalets*. Raised in Australia, Barbara studied in Sydney at the School of Interior Design. Although Barbara continues with freelance projects, she devotes much of her time to illustrating Karen's Country Inn guides. Barbara lives in the San Francisco Bay area with her husband, Richard, and their three children.